BVRB'S

COMMODES

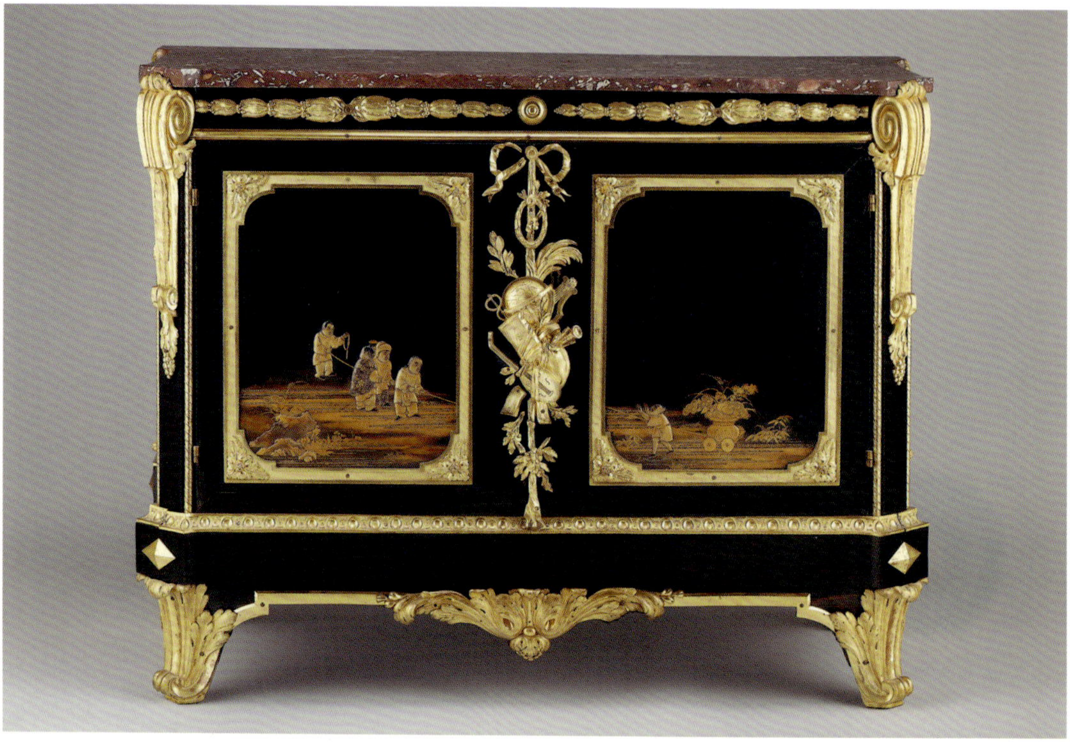

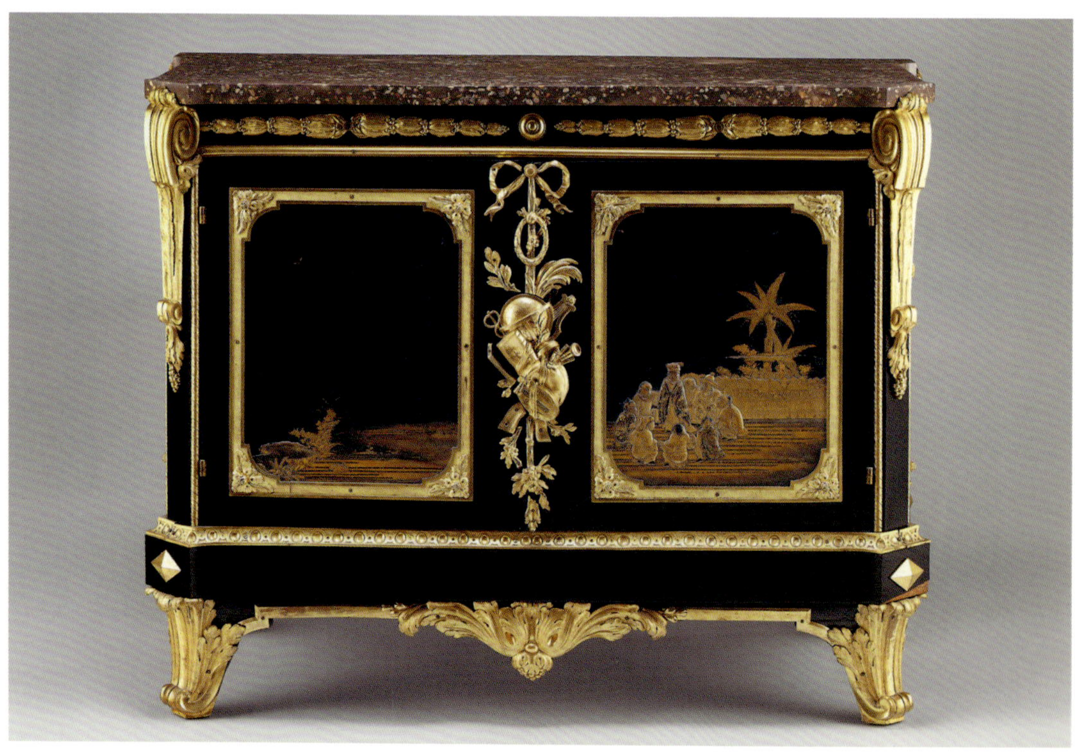

BVRB'S COMMODES

Marie-Laure Buku Pongo

William Christie

The Frick Collection, New York
in association with D Giles Limited

FRICK DIPTYCH SERIES

Designed to foster critical engagement and interest specialist and non-specialist alike, each book in this series illuminates a single work in the Frick's rich collection with an essay by a Frick curator paired with a contribution from a contemporary artist or writer.

First published in 2025 by The Frick Collection
1 East 70th Street
New York, NY 10021
www.frick.org

Michaelyn Mitchell, Editor in Chief
Gemma McElroy, Assistant Editor

In association with GILES
An imprint of D Giles Limited
66 High Street
Lewes, BN7 1XG, UK
gilesltd.com

EU GPSR authorised representative
LOGOS EUROPE, 9 rue Nicolas Poussin, 17000,
La Rochelle, France
E-mail: contact@logoseurope.eu

Copyedited and proofread by Sarah Kane
Designed by Caroline and Roger Hillier,
The Old Chapel Graphic Design

Typeset in Garamond
Produced by GILES
Printed and bound in China

A CIP catalogue record for this book is available from the Library of Congress.

ISBN 978-1-917273-12-1

Cover and page 18: detail from Bernard van Risenburgh II and Bernard van Risenburgh III, *Pair of Commodes*, ca. 1764 (frontispiece)

Frontispiece: Bernard van Risenburgh II and Bernard van Risenburgh III, *Pair of Commodes*, ca. 1764. Oak with veneered ebony, tulipwood, amaranth, and padouk, lacquer, gilt bronze, porphyry, marble, h. 35 ¼ in. (89.5 cm), l. 47 ¼ in. (120 cm), w. 22 in. (55.9 cm). The Frick Collection, New York

Distributed in the USA and Canada by
Consortium Book Sales & Distribution
The Keg House
34 Thirteenth Avenue, NE, Suite 101
Minneapolis, MN 55413-1007
USA
www.cbsd.com

CONTENTS

Bernard van Risenburgh II (ca. 1696–ca. 1766) and his son Bernard van Risenburgh III (act. 1764–ca. 1800) are part of a dynasty of extraordinary cabinetmakers, and the Frick's commodes by them—probably begun by the father and completed by the son—are jewels in the crown of our decorative arts collection. With the four exquisite Japanese lacquer panels incorporated into each piece, the pair of commodes reflects the eighteenth-century taste throughout Europe for chinoiseries, among the subjects addressed by Marie-Laure Buku Pongo, Associate Curator of Decorative Arts, in her absorbing text. The taste for chinoiserie extended to all the arts, including music. In his engaging essay, the revered conductor and keyboardist William Christie discusses his "chinoiseries passion" and its manifestation in his home and instruments. We are most grateful to them both for their contributions to this publication.

Thanks also go to Editor in Chief Michaelyn Mitchell, who coordinated the production of the publication and, with Assistant Editor Gemma McElroy, edited the text; as well as to Joseph Coscia Jr., who captured such beautiful images of the commodes and the subtleties of the lacquer details. We would also like to express our gratitude to our publishing partner, D Giles Limited.

Axel Rüger
Anna-Maria and Stephen Kellen Director, The Frick Collection

ACKNOWLEDGMENTS

First and foremost, I would like to thank William Christie for enthusiastically agreeing to contribute to this publication. It was through his wonderful recordings of Lully, Charpentier, Couperin, and Rameau with Les Arts Florissants, the early-music ensemble he founded in 1979, that I first learned of the extraordinary musicians who lived during the reign of Louis XIV and contributed so much to the culture of France in the seventeenth and eighteenth centuries. I am always grateful to Michaelyn Mitchell, Editor in Chief, for managing the incredible Diptych series, of which this book is volume sixteen, and editing it so capably with Gemma McElroy, Assistant Editor. I am indebted to Ian Wardropper, the former Anna-Maria and Stephen Kellen Director, and Xavier F. Salomon, Deputy Director and Peter Jay Sharp Chief Curator, for their support of my projects and ideas, as well as to my colleagues Aimee Ng and Giulio Dalvit, for their steadfast encouragement. I would like to acknowledge the contribution of Joseph Godla, former Chief Conservator, as well as Pat King, Head of Preparation and Installation, and the Frick's photographer, Joseph Coscia Jr., who captured these wonderful pieces with his lens.

I am extremely grateful to a number of others who discussed with me French lacquer furniture and allowed me to study several pieces, particularly Jenny Saunt at the Victoria and Albert Museum; Daniëlle Kisluk-Grosheide at the Metropolitan Museum of Art; Émile Van Binnebeke and Vincent Cattersel at the Musée Royal d'Art et d'Histoire du Cinquantenaire; and Grace Chuang, who shared valuable archival material on the Van Risenburgh dynasty. My gratitude also goes to Stéphane Castelluccio, who was one of my PhD supervisors. Stéphane has written extensively on the taste for lacquerware during the ancien régime, and he and I have had many discussions over the last few years. Finally, I would like to thank a number of individuals who were my colleagues at Versailles: Yves Carlier, Chief Curator and Head of the Decorative Arts Department, who helped me to obtain a number of images; Bertrand Rondot, with whom I discussed the project; and finally Christine Desgrez, who welcomed me warmly at the library of the Château de Versailles to look at documents related to their furniture by Van Risenburgh II.

Marie-Laure Buku Pongo
Associate Curator of Decorative Arts, The Frick Collection

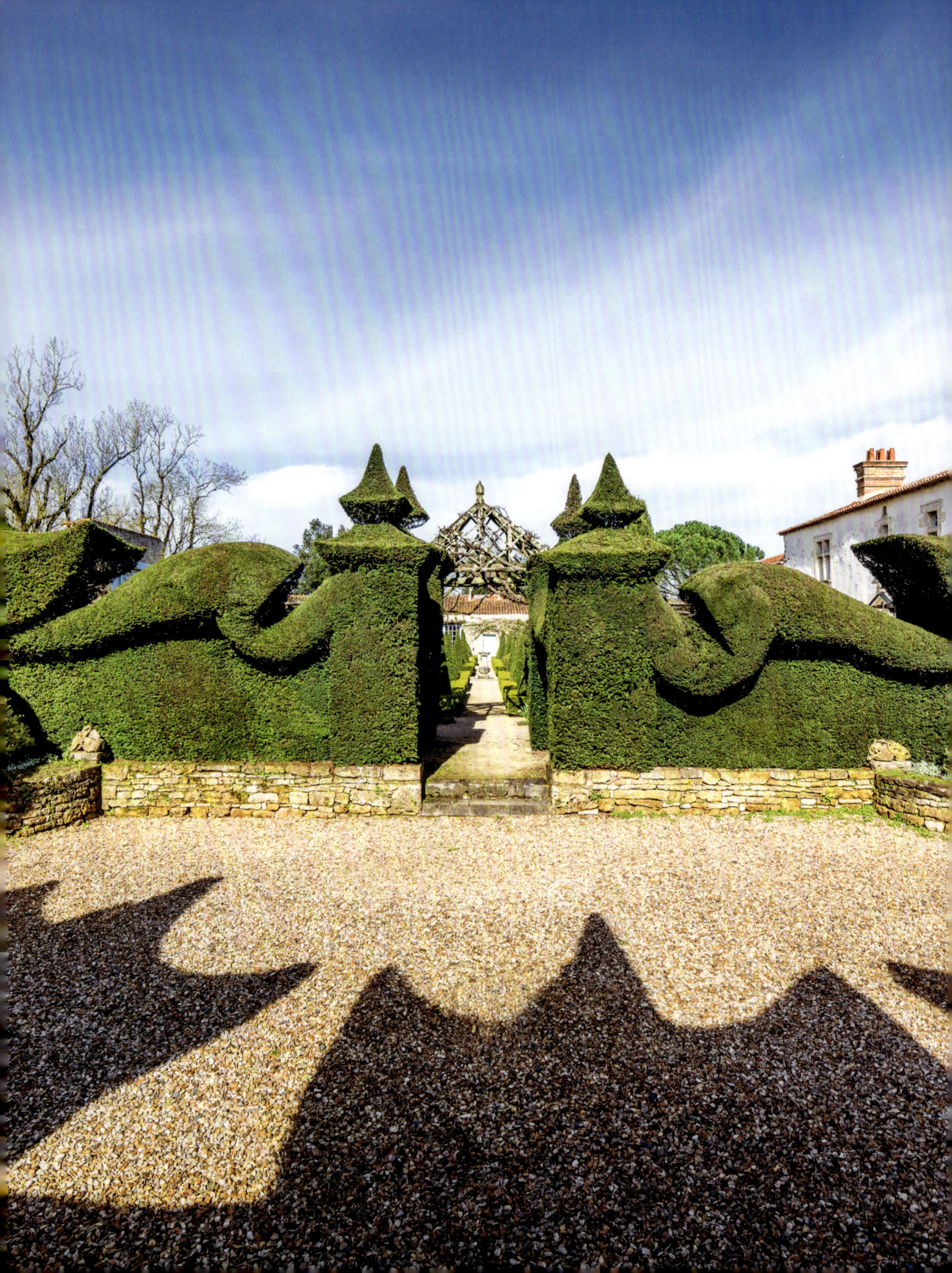

VAN RISENBURGH, A HARPSICHORD, AND A HENHOUSE

William Christie

In 2004, I traveled to the Shanghai Grand Theatre with the musicians of my ensemble Les Arts Florissants to perform *Les Paladins*, a *comédie lyrique* by Jean-Philippe Rameau. Presenting in China an eighteenth-century French opera that not only had never been performed outside of France but had completely disappeared from the Parisian stage for more than two centuries was quite unusual and extravagant! In the third act of *Les Paladins*, the fairy Manto sows confusion in the mind of another character, the perfidious Anselme, by magically transforming the setting of the action, a medieval castle, into a pagoda. The entire plot then unfolds in this space, animated by dancers and singers costumed in a way to create the illusion of a palace of the Celestial Empire. So there we were, bringing to China a piece of musical chinoiserie, reviving a work that mirrored eighteenth-century Europe's fascination with a dreamed-of China—in front of a twenty-first-century Chinese audience!

Chinoiserie is fantasy. It was born of the West's fascination with a distant and make-believe China. For many centuries, European artists have responded to the allure of an imaginary East, letting their creativity wander and giving rise to oftentimes extraordinary art. This mania is found everywhere in Europe, flourishing especially in the seventeenth and eighteenth centuries. In France, the chinoiserie decorations by an artist such as Jean-Antoine Watteau had a profound influence across Europe, far beyond the artist's own generation.

Chinoiserie extended to all the arts. Music, of course, is no exception, and *Les Paladins* is not an isolated case. Throughout the baroque period, European composers succumbed to this China mania, producing myriad musical pieces inlaid with chinoiserie themes. In England, Henry Purcell finishes off his

The author's *théâtre de verdure*, Vendée, France

Fairy Queen (1692) with a Chinese tableau involving two Chinese characters. France was particularly rich in musical chinoiserie: François Couperin's harpsichord piece *Les Chinois* (1730) comes to mind, and, in the operatic world, Charles-Simon Favart's *Noces chinoises* (1756), André-Ernest Modeste Grétry's *Panurge dans l'île des lanternes* (1785), and Christoph Willibald Gluck's *Les Chinoises* (1754).

Were French composers familiar with real Chinese music? I think the answer is no. French scholars of the eighteenth century did publish learned works on Chinese music, but this intellectual accuracy was not shared by composers. There is nothing Chinese about the music of *Les Paladins*. Asia appears merely as a dramatic expedient, of a purely cosmetic nature, to bring an exotic ornament to staged music. But Rameau, like the artists of his time, nonetheless took immense pleasure in integrating this aesthetic influence into his Western creativity. Above all, what we see here is a European gaze, charged with fuzzy fascination.

The Frick's two Van Risenburgh commodes, created around 1764, are roughly contemporary with *Les Paladins*, which was first performed just four years before. These objects are of stunning majesty, at once sober and precious—an emblem of luxury as it was practiced in the great houses of the eighteenth century. I see here the encounter between two worlds—Asia and Europe—two creations by an illustrious French family of cabinetmakers, the Van Risenburghs, and eight panels of exquisite lacquerwork, created by extraordinary yet unknown Japanese artists, probably a century earlier.

These two pieces of furniture are not, strictly speaking, chinoiseries. We are not dealing with pure fantasy born of the imagination of a European artist. Asia manifests itself here with its own voice. By incorporating Japanese lacquer into European-style furniture, the Van Risenburghs placed Asian works of art into a Western context, much like a jeweler setting a precious stone or a French decorator surrounding Chinese porcelain with bronze ormolu mounts.

I like to think that the Frick commodes suggest a mark of immense respect on the part of the Van Risenburghs. Other furniture of this dynasty's cabinetwork shows less respect for Chinese or Japanese lacquer: here, two great *ébénistes*—father and son—seem to pay homage to what they have borrowed from the East. They use rich but discreet veneering of ebony and other precious woods to enhance the Japanese lacquer, and only the exquisite gilt-bronze ornamentation evokes the opulence of French *ébénisterie*.

What was the Van Risenburghs' appreciation of these eight Japanese panels? Were the panels considered comparable to their own art, or even superior? The beauty of these Frick commodes is the confrontation of two aesthetics and the ways they enrich each other, bringing a profound elegance to the ensemble.

The real, the fake . . . Of course, the creative process for the Frick commodes was not the same as that for the music of Rameau. But both tell us something about their time, illustrating the spirit of curiosity that pervades eighteenth-century French culture. For myself, I oscillate between fake and real. I love "make-believe Orientalia." Perhaps a brief journey down memory lane is in order here—memories of growing up with a fascination for things Chinese. One of my first memories of this dates back to my early teens. I recall being absorbed in the contemplation of a plate at my grandmother's house—a nineteenth-century English blue and white transfer plate that depicted a weeping willow and a fisherman. I made a drawing of the scene to make it my own. In the years following, I began collecting some real Chinese objects—a glass snuff bottle, a red lacquer bowl, a Kangxi plate, and a few textiles— but also, over time, some fakes, very desirable chinoiseries: seventeenth- and eighteenth-century delftware.

And then, cuisine. As my friends well know, cooking is one of my passions. I remember the day my father brought home Chinese take-out for us children, from Buffalo's only Chinese restaurant. My first Chinese meal! Years later, I was able to spend time in the kitchen of a well-known Chinese restaurant in New Haven, Connecticut, which had a rather lovely name: Blessings. It specialized in northern, Peking-style cuisine. These moments were almost as important as my studies at Yale School of Music. I have never stopped cooking, nor have I stopped collecting Asian art. As I write this text, I am looking at a large Japanese teapot with metal mounts, probably dating to the early eighteenth century.

My passion for collecting and my aesthetic taste are best seen in and around my country home in the Vendée. In 1985, I was fortunate to be able to buy a manor house in western France dating from the early seventeenth century. I have since completely restored it to its original beauty. Inside, you will find furniture, musical instruments, and a painting collection (including a portrait gallery), as well as a fairly extensive collection of Chinese porcelain, mainly from the eighteenth and nineteenth centuries, alongside my collection of delftware. But it is outside that I let my imagination run wild. Since the mid-80s, I have created, from scratch, a rather large garden, divided into different areas with very evident references to my chinoiseries passion. There are Chinese bridges, one placed beside a magnificent weeping willow, though without the fisherman of Grandma's plate (facing page). There is also a henhouse of my own design (below), in the shape of a small pagoda. The kitchen garden and the potting sheds are surrounded by chestnut slat fences, the interlacing of which echoes Chinese decorative motifs.

The most emblematic piece of what I like to call this "rustic chinoiserie" is undoubtedly my green theater, my *théâtre de verdure* (page 8). When I planted the young yews, more than thirty years ago, I already had in mind the shape

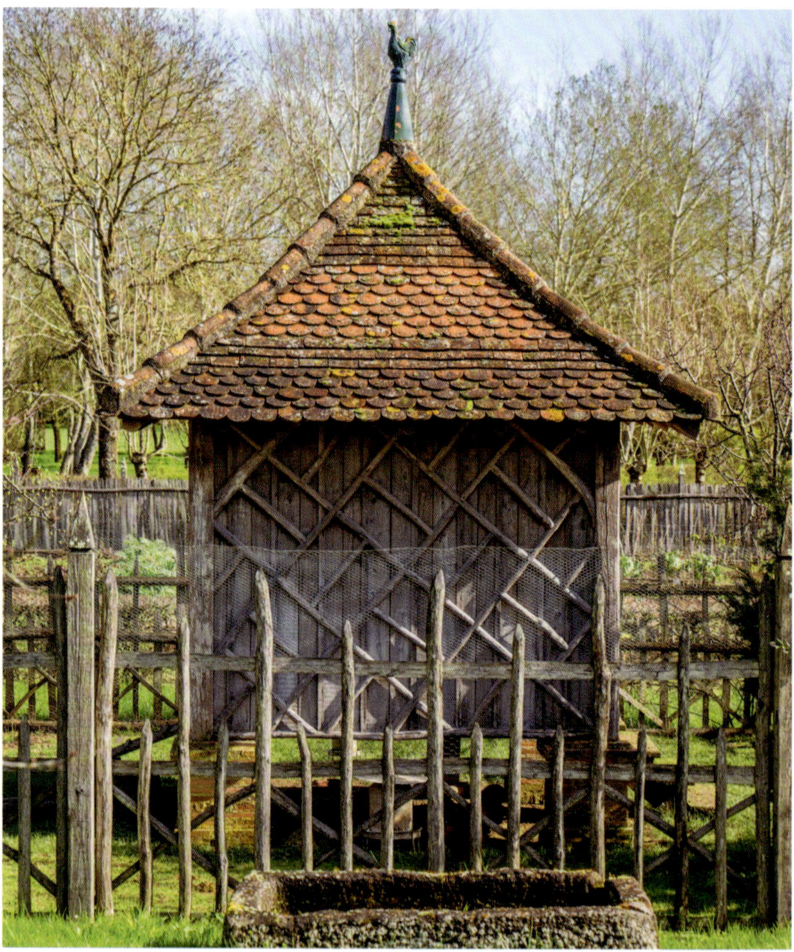

Henhouse in the author's gardens, Vendée, France, 2024

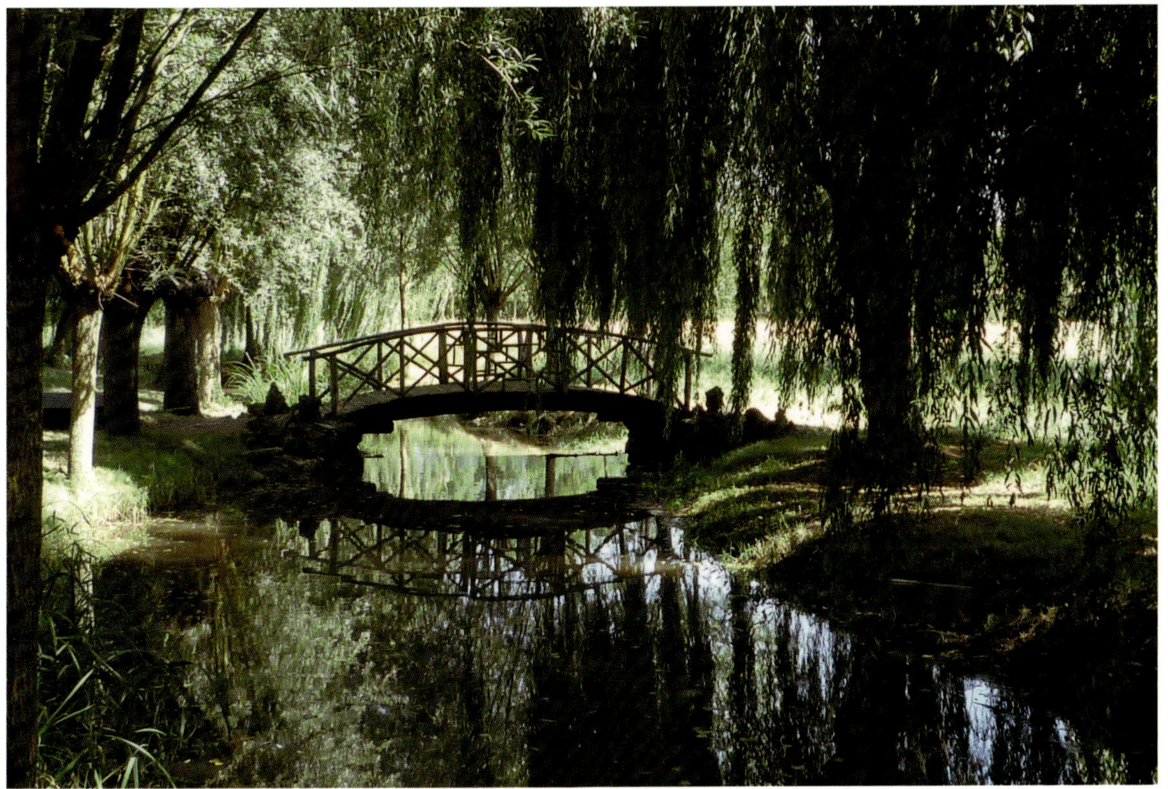

Chinese bridge in the author's gardens, Vendée, France, 2012

I wanted to give to this vegetal architecture—that of a large Chinese pagoda. A true *Paladins* set! It is an extravagant realization and a bit of a nightmare for the gardeners who must clip and prune it every year.

I think of my garden as a utopia where everything I love, everything that moves me, comes together in a blend of places, styles, eras, and, above all, sensations. Its chinoiserie represents a dreamy, faraway Arcadia with omnipresent nature—an imaginary world filled with exotic animals, happy children, fantastical architecture, elegant courtesans, and happy fishermen.

The original owner of the Van Risenburgh commodes is unknown. But I imagine that we have something in common. Perhaps he—or she—was an amateur musician, as were many of his social class. He could have played the harpsichord or the violin or the viola da gamba or could have simply listened to music in the room where these two cabinets were placed. Perhaps he even had the chance to hear Rameau's *Les Paladins* at the Académie Royale de Musique or to have its most appreciated melodies played in his salon!

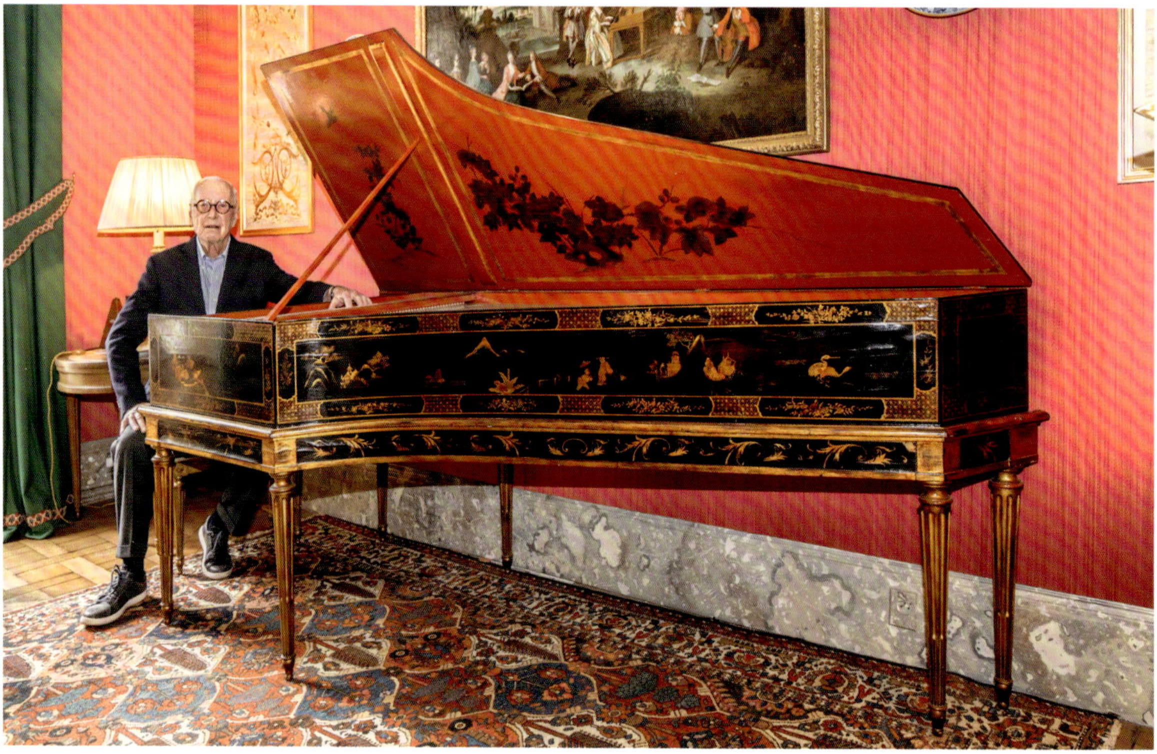

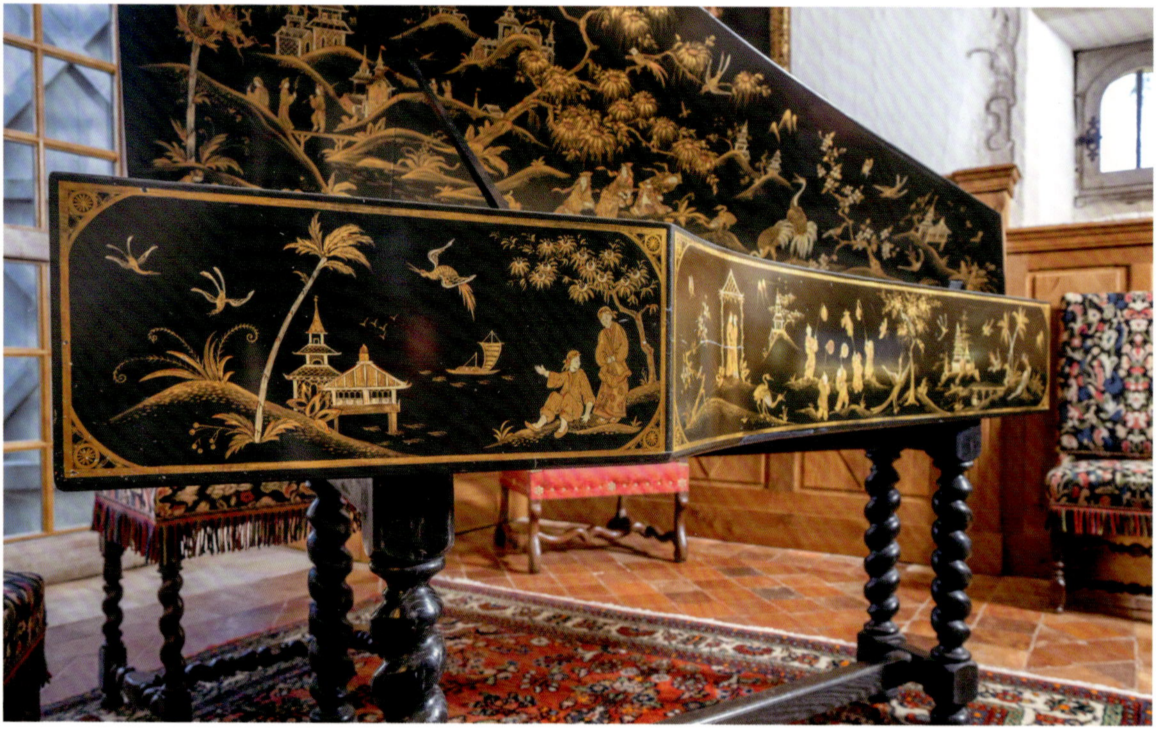

Can music be visual? Can one see music? And what do we hear when we look? This reflection inevitably brings me back to my instrument, the harpsichord. Unlike modern pianos, it was not only made to produce sounds. It was a much-admired piece of furniture, considered a work of art. Of course, it is an object that must be considered for its musical qualities, but it is also one that charms the eye as much as the ear. Harpsichords of the seventeenth and eighteenth centuries benefited from the chinoiserie mania. The examples of highly decorated instruments in Chinese taste are to be found all over Europe in the baroque period.

A personal story. In 1970, when I was twenty-six, I moved from the United States to France—undoubtedly one of the most decisive moments of my life. One of my first purchases to accompany me in this new life was a harpsichord. I was fortunate to know an American instrument maker, William Dowd, who had just set up shop in Paris. There was much talk about how the harpsichord would be embellished. I had dreamt for a very long time of an instrument in chinoiserie and was able to find a decorator established in the Faubourg Saint-Antoine who specialized in the eighteenth-century decorating techniques and styles. My instrument emerged from his atelier several months later, splendidly ornamented in Vernis Martin chinoiserie, beautiful imitations of eighteenth-century lacquer (facing page, top). This harpsichord, built in 1971, continues to share my life. I also own a second instrument built by another American maker, Willard Martin, and acquired a few years later, which also boasts splendid chinoiserie decorations (facing page, bottom).

There is a third harpsichord that has been a faithful and treasured friend for many years. I am as close to it as I am to the two that I own. Housed in the Musée de la Musique at the Philharmonie de Paris, it is a sumptuous instrument that was made in the first half of the eighteenth century by a Parisian maker, Jean-Claude Goujon, and decorated in Vernis Martin chinoiseries (page 16). It is indeed one of the most beautiful instruments to listen to and look at. I gained a new appreciation for this harpsichord most recently, dating from the moment when Xavier Salomon asked whether I might enjoy writing about the Van Risenburgh commodes. Very simply stated, the Goujon harpsichord bears an extraordinary resemblance to the Van Risenburgh furniture (pages 16, 17). The decorating techniques are obviously very different: Van Risenburgh's respectful homage to an art from Asia on the one hand, and a reinvention in chinoiserie by a Parisian decorator on the

The author at his harpsichord made by William Dowd

The author's harpsichord made by Willard Martin

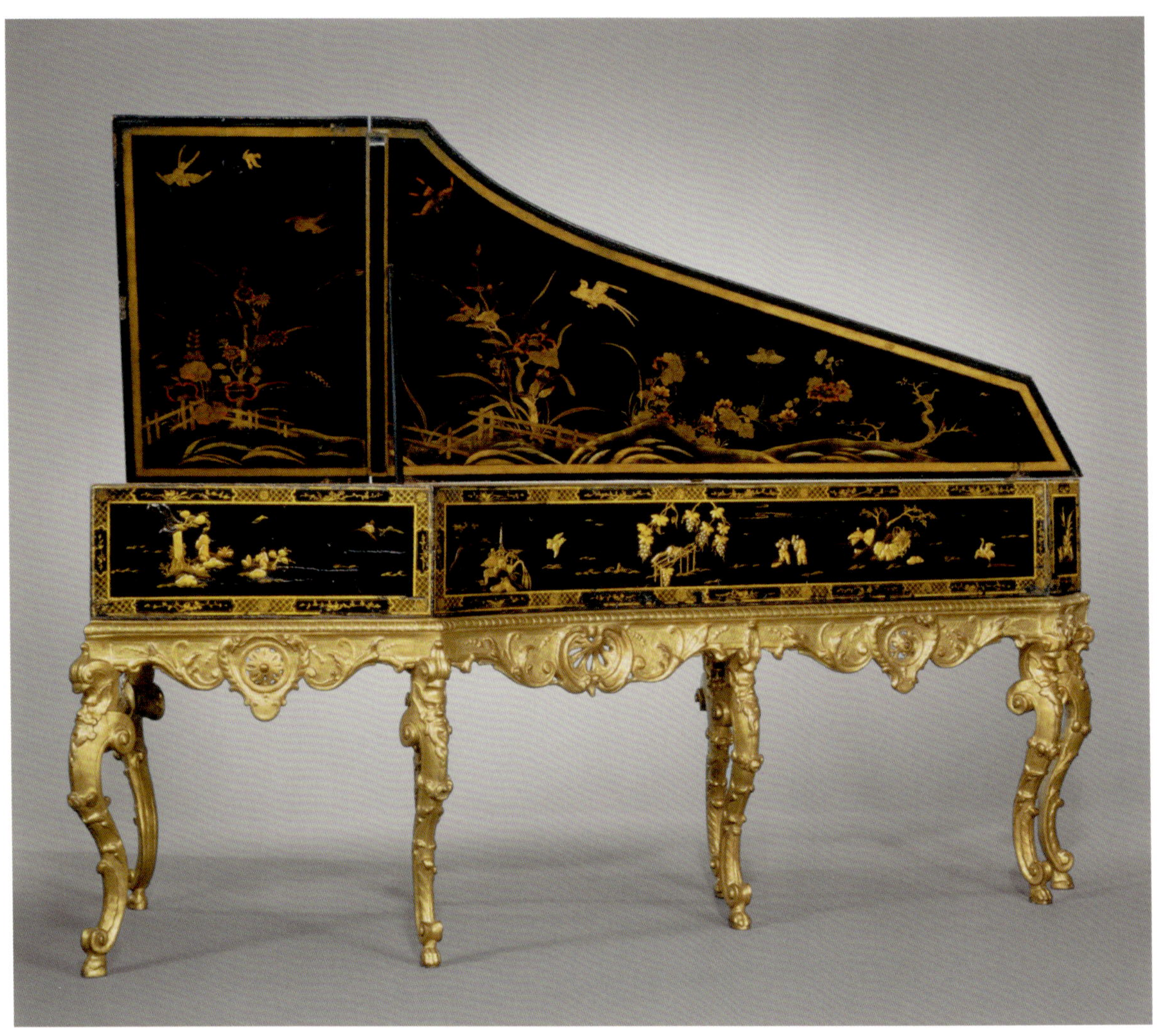

Harpsichord made by Jean-Claude Goujon, 1st half of 18th century. Musée de la Musique, Paris

other. Yet, these different objects share the aesthetic qualities of sobriety and richness and inspire the same emotional response. These visual similarities are almost unsettling. Since my association with the Frick commodes, I have dreamt of seeing the objects together. The commodes are mute and give us exquisite visual pleasure; the Goujon harpsichord can excite the eye, but how extraordinary is the phenomenon that it can also speak to us! All of these objects, essentially, provide the same aesthetic pleasures that have nourished me for so many years, and it is with this feeling of happiness that I finish this small homage to the Frick commodes.

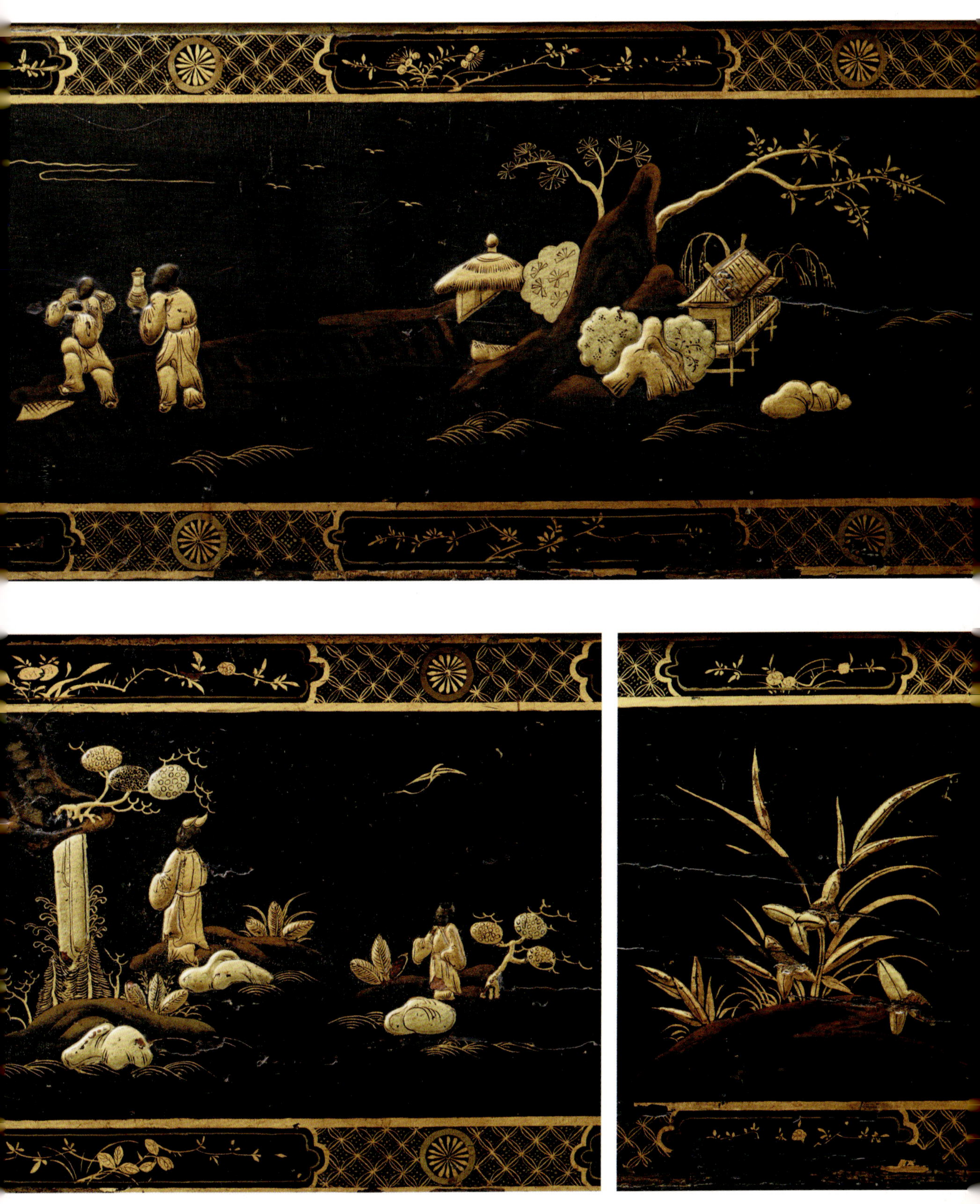

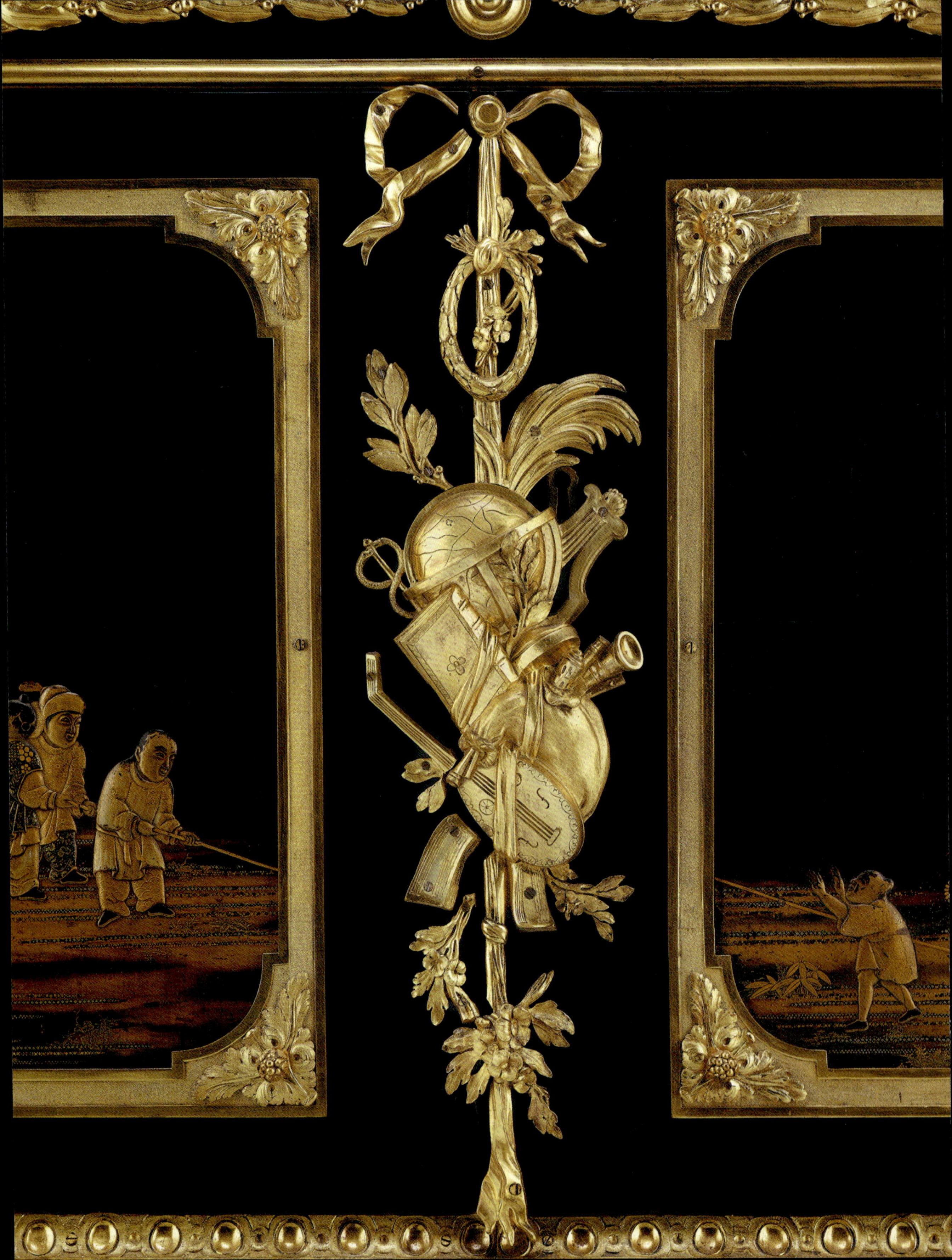

BVRB'S COMMODES

Marie-Laure Buku Pongo

The *sieur* Gersaint is particularly keen to collect everything of interest that China and Japan can provide . . . that is most pleasing; he is also supplied with several useful goods . . . in the latest taste and from the best manufacturers.
—*Mercure de France*, October 1740

While at the Musée des Beaux-Arts in Dijon in September 2024, I came across the "presumed" portrait of the Dijon-born composer Jean-Philippe Rameau (1683–1764) (fig. 1). Shortly thereafter, as I was wandering around the old part of the city before my next appointment, I found myself in front of a sculpture of Rameau after Eugène Guillaume outside the Dijon Conservatory (fig. 2).[1] These two depictions of the composer brought to mind the gilt-bronze musical instruments that adorn a pair of commodes *à vantaux* (with two doors) by Bernard van Risenburgh II (ca. 1696–ca. 1766) and his son Bernard van Risenburgh III (act. 1764–ca. 1800) that reside in the Frick's Living Hall under the watchful eyes of Hans Holbein's *Sir Thomas More* and *Thomas Cromwell*. As I pictured these pieces, I felt I could hear the music of Rameau's opera-ballet *Les Indes galantes* (The Amorous Indies).

Contemporaries who gained renown among the aristocracy and the royal family, Bernard van Risenburgh II and Rameau both fell into obscurity at the end of the ancien régime. Rameau's music was rediscovered many years later by a generation of musicians and conductors—William Christie (who recorded *Les Indes galantes* in 1991), Roger Norrington, John Eliot Gardiner, Marc Minkowski, Simon Rattle, Jordi Savall, and Christophe Rousset—who recorded his work and that of many of his contemporaries. It was not until 1975 that his *Les Boréades*, a five-act *tragédie en musique* (musical tragedy) composed around 1763, was presented to the public for the first time.[2] Other works by Rameau—among the most popular in the eighteenth century—received a similar treatment: *Les Indes galantes* was presented in its entirety again in 1957 at the Opéra Royal in Versailles. As for Van Risenburgh, he was rediscovered that same year with the publication of an article that identified him as the cabinetmaker who stamped his work with the letters BVRB.[3]

Les Indes galantes was first presented in Paris on August 23, 1735.[4] The opera-ballet is said to have been inspired by the diplomatic visit to France of a delegation of five Native Americans, who performed their traditional dances at the Comédie-Italienne in Paris.[5] In a letter of October 1727 to the academician Antoine Houdart de la Motte, Rameau wrote that he was inspired by their performance to compose *Les Sauvages* (The Savages) in 1725 for his *Nouvelles suites de pièces de clavecin* (New Pieces for Harpsichord), which he mostly reused for the fourth act of *Les Indes galantes*.[6] The representatives came

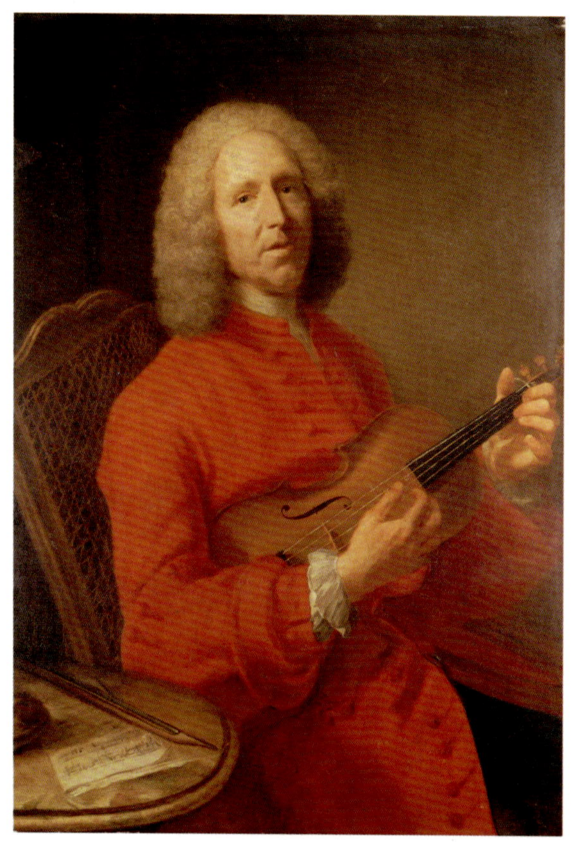

Fig. 1
Attributed to Joseph Aved
Presumed Portrait of Jean-Philippe Rameau, ca. 1728
Oil on canvas
46 1/16 × 32 3/4 in. (117 × 83 cm)
Musée des Beaux-Arts, Dijon

from Louisiana, a vast territory under French rule that stretched from the Great Lakes region to the Gulf of Mexico. Louis XV had received them in November 1725 at Fontainebleau, where he was spending time away from Versailles after his recent marriage to Maria Leszczyńska, the daughter of the dethroned king of Poland, Stanisław Leszczyński.[7] Like most non-European embassies or delegations, the group visited the Invalides, the Opéra, Versailles, the Ménagerie, Trianon, and Marly—a practice begun during the reign of Louis XIV—before their formal introduction to the king.[8]

Parisians were fascinated by the Native American men. Their physical appearance, their attire, and their dances were recounted in periodicals such as the *Mercure de France*.[9] Agapit Chicagou, leader of the Mitchigamea, in particular, was described as a beautiful man. It is important to underscore that in the eighteenth century, the term "Indian"—as used in *Les Indes galantes* and elsewhere—typically referred to anyone living outside Europe, whether from the Americas, Africa, or Asia. Louis Fuzelier's libretto for *Les Indes galantes* includes scenes and events set in the Ottoman Empire, Persia, and Peru.[10] In large part, the rising use of Japanese and Chinese lacquer on furniture (like the commodes at the Frick) and small objects (such as snuffboxes) has its origins in the European fascination with the "other," a concept replete with what we consider today to be negative stereotypes.[11] Nonetheless, the Frick's exquisite commodes remain an intriguing example of the cultural exchange in the eighteenth century between Europe and Asia.

Two Commodes *à vantaux*

In 1918, Henry Clay Frick acquired the pair of commodes stamped BVRB and JME (fig. 3) —the monogram used by the Jurande des Menuisiers-Ébénistes, the guild of wood carvers and cabinetmakers that controlled the quality of the work of its members—toward the end of his life. Frick bought the commodes from the dealer Joseph Duveen (1869–1939), who had previously sold him numerous decorative arts objects and pieces of furniture. In 1915, for example, Frick had purchased from Duveen a mechanical table with porcelain plaques by the eighteenth-century cabinetmaker Martin Carlin (ca. 1730–1785), as well as a commode made by Roger Vandercruse Lacroix (1728–1799) known as RVLC, under the direction of Gilles Joubert (1689–1775) for the bedroom of Madame Victoire (1733–1799), daughter of Louis XV, at the Château de Compiègne. A year later, Frick acquired a pair of octagonal pedestals and a *Bureau plat à huit pieds* (kneehole desk) by André-Charles Boulle (1642–1732). The pair of BVRB commodes came from an English collection, as confirmed by a label affixed by Duveen to the inner door of both pieces, which bears the following inscription:

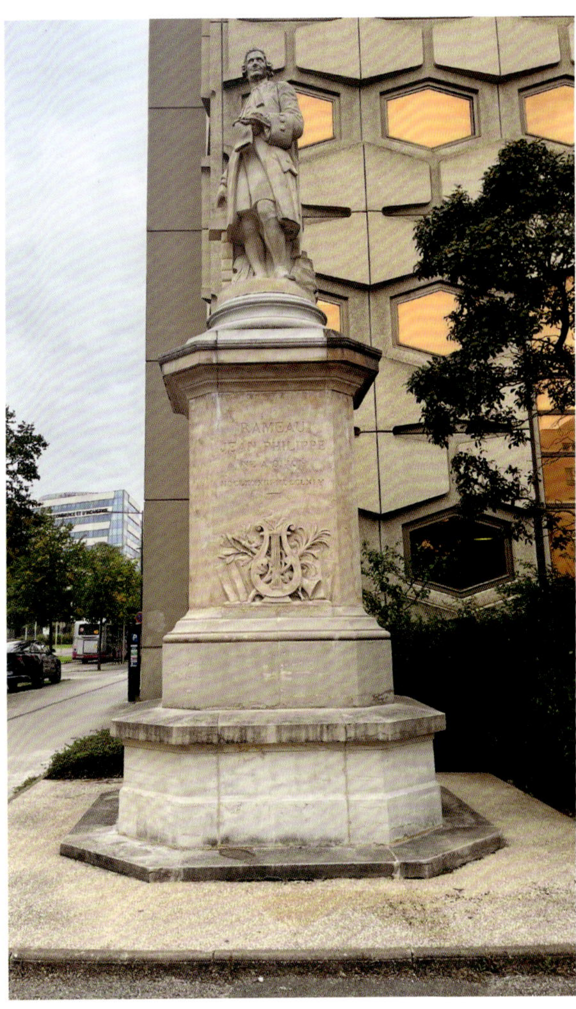

Fig. 2
After Eugène Guillaume,
Monument to Jean-Philippe
Rameau, ca. 1950
Stone, h. 98½ in. (250 cm)
Boulevard Georges Clemenceau,
Dijon

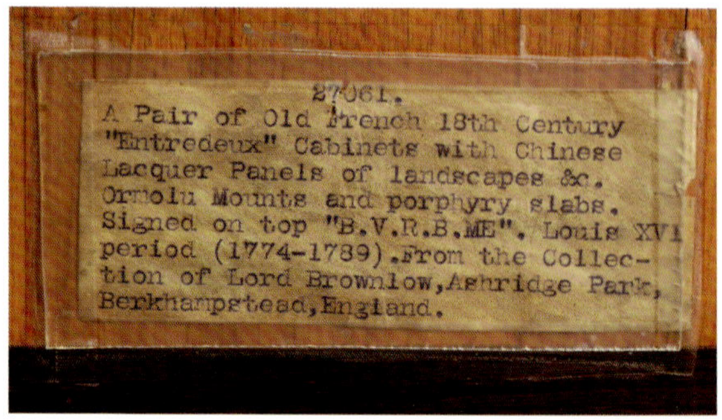

Fig. 3
Detail of *Pair of Commodes*
(frontispiece), showing stamp

Fig. 4
Detail of *Pair of Commodes*
(frontispiece), showing label
inside of door

27061. A Pair of Old French 18th Century "Entredeux" Cabinets with Chinese Lacquer Panels of landscapes &c. Ormolu mounts and porphyry slabs. Signed on top "B.V.R.B.[J]ME." Louis XVI period (1774–1789). From the Collec-tion of Lord Brownlow, Ashridge Park, Berkhampstead [*sic*], England [fig. 4].

The provenance of the commodes before Adelbert Wellington Brownlow (1844–1921), 3rd Earl Brownlow, is unknown. They appeared in an 1803 anonymous sale in Paris, the catalogue of which was written by prominent dealer and auctioneer Alexandre Joseph Paillet (1743–1814) and Grégoire-Hippolyte Delaroche (1761–1839). Among the paintings, drawings, porcelains, bronzes, and other works of art, the commodes are described under the number 342: "Two rich Bas d'armoire (low cabinets) . . . each opening on two sides, decorated with Japanese lacquer panels with Chinese figures, plants, and shrubs in relief and gold on black ground. They are adorned with various ornaments of good taste, such as an upside-down console, [an] oak garland, music trophies . . . all in well-chased bronze and gilded. . . . Their tops are of Tarentais marble, one of which is stapled."[12] Each commode is a rectangular case made of oak—a wood often used in fine eighteenth-century furniture—and canted at the four corners, with a single shelf behind two doors. Most of the structural elements are connected by an *assemblage à queue d'aronde* (dovetail joint) or secured with dowels (fig. 5). They are extensively described by Theodore Dell in his catalogue on furniture at the Frick.[13]

The main structural elements are: the four stiles; three upper front and side rails [are] set horizontally and joined to the tops of the stiles with double dovetails in front and single dovetails at rear . . . three lower front and side rails [have] their joints hidden from view but probably consisting of dowelled tenons.[14]

With the exception of the interiors, which are unfinished, the cabinets are veneered with exotic woods. The fronts and sides are veneered with ebony painted black for a richer appearance. The doors have panels of tulipwood banded with amaranth and framed with padouk, a tropical wood from sub-Saharan Africa. The commodes are richly decorated with gilt bronzes that also provide protection, especially at the corners and the feet. The bronzes feature a variety of motifs, from acanthus foliage, laurel leaves, and berries with a ribbon along the friezes to emblems of the arts and sciences—a terrestrial globe, a lyre, a book, a horn, a lute, and a sheet of music.

The four black-and-gold Japanese lacquer panels on the front and sides of each commode are of exceptional quality and were probably made a century earlier. Decorated with landscapes—a continuous scene across the doors that form the front of the commodes—they depict men and women engaging in various activities. On the front of one commode (fig. 6), four seemingly well-dressed men are pulling a rope tied to a cart that contains a large urn with flowers. Another figure—likely a gardener—appears to be directing the operation. The scene on the two front panels of the other commode (fig. 7) depicts eight men and women (also seemingly well-dressed) listening to a man standing in their midst. The scene is set in a landscape composed of plants, flowers, and rocks. Similar landscapes are on the sides of the panels. Several techniques were used to make these intricate scenes. The cart, rocks, and houses depicted on one commode, as well as the trees, rocks, and vegetal elements represented on the other, are all executed in *takamakie*, a Japanese lacquerwork method that creates raised areas surfaced with gold powder. The ground and mottled gold-and-brown areas are done in *hiramakie*, which also uses powdered gold but on a flat lacquered surface. The horizontal lines and ridges that appear to cross the ground are in *okibirame*, a technique in which small flakes of silver and gold foil are inlaid. The human figures—in high relief on both cabinets—are mostly done in *sabi-age-takamakie* (which uses gold powder), whereas their lavish clothes include flecks of mother-of-pearl arranged in mosaic patterns (*aogai*).[15] Finally, each piece of furniture is topped with a slab of porphyry marble, a highly prized stone used during antiquity by Roman emperors.

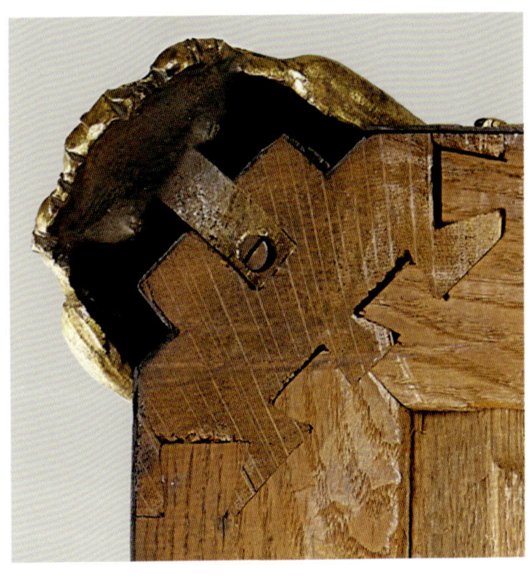

Fig. 5
Detail of *Pair of Commodes* (frontispiece), showing the dovetail joint assemblage

Fig. 6 (pages 24–27)
Details of *Pair of Commodes* (frontispiece, top), showing the lacquer panels

Fig. 7 (pages 28–31)
Details of *Pair of Commodes* (frontispiece, bottom), showing the lacquer panels

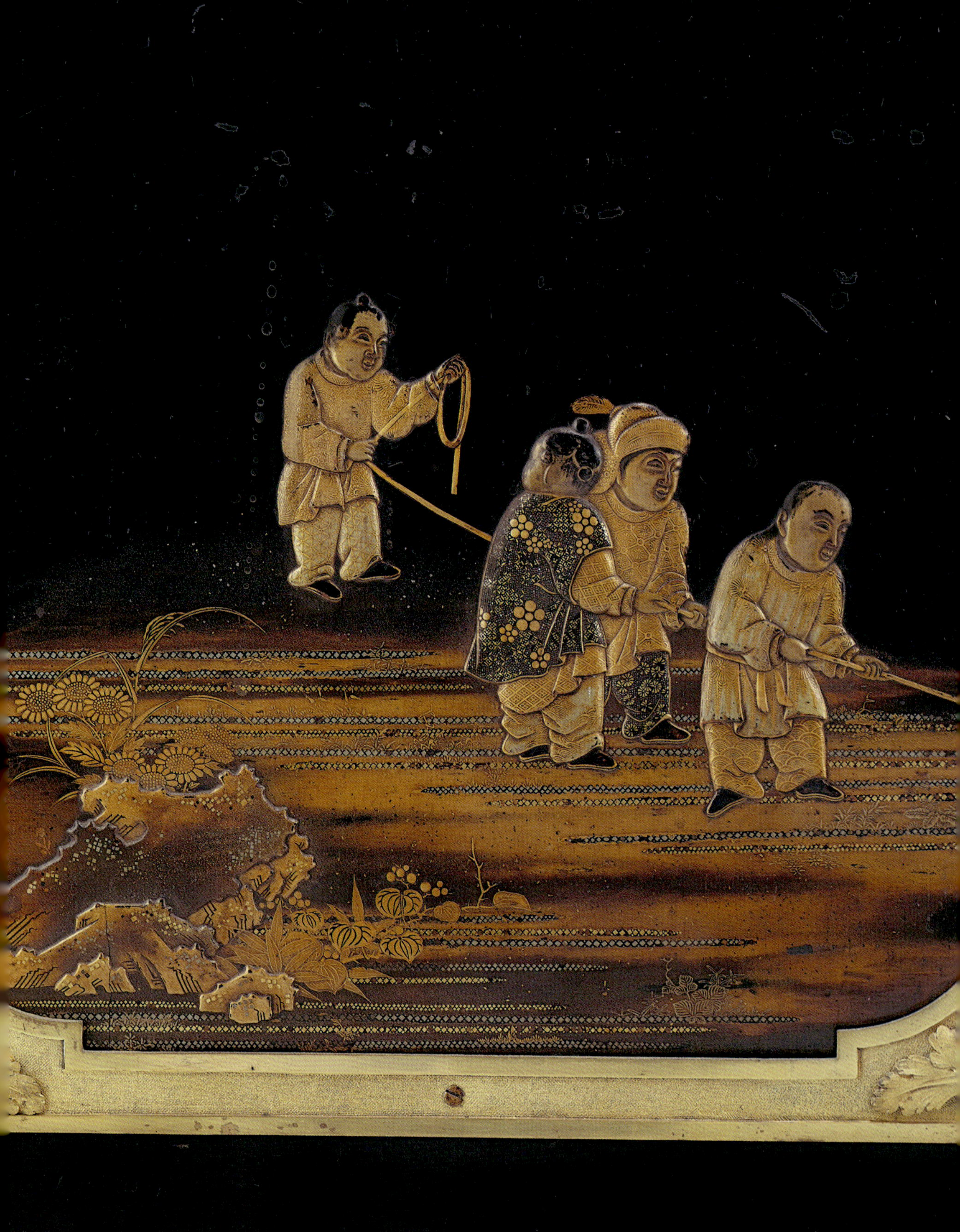

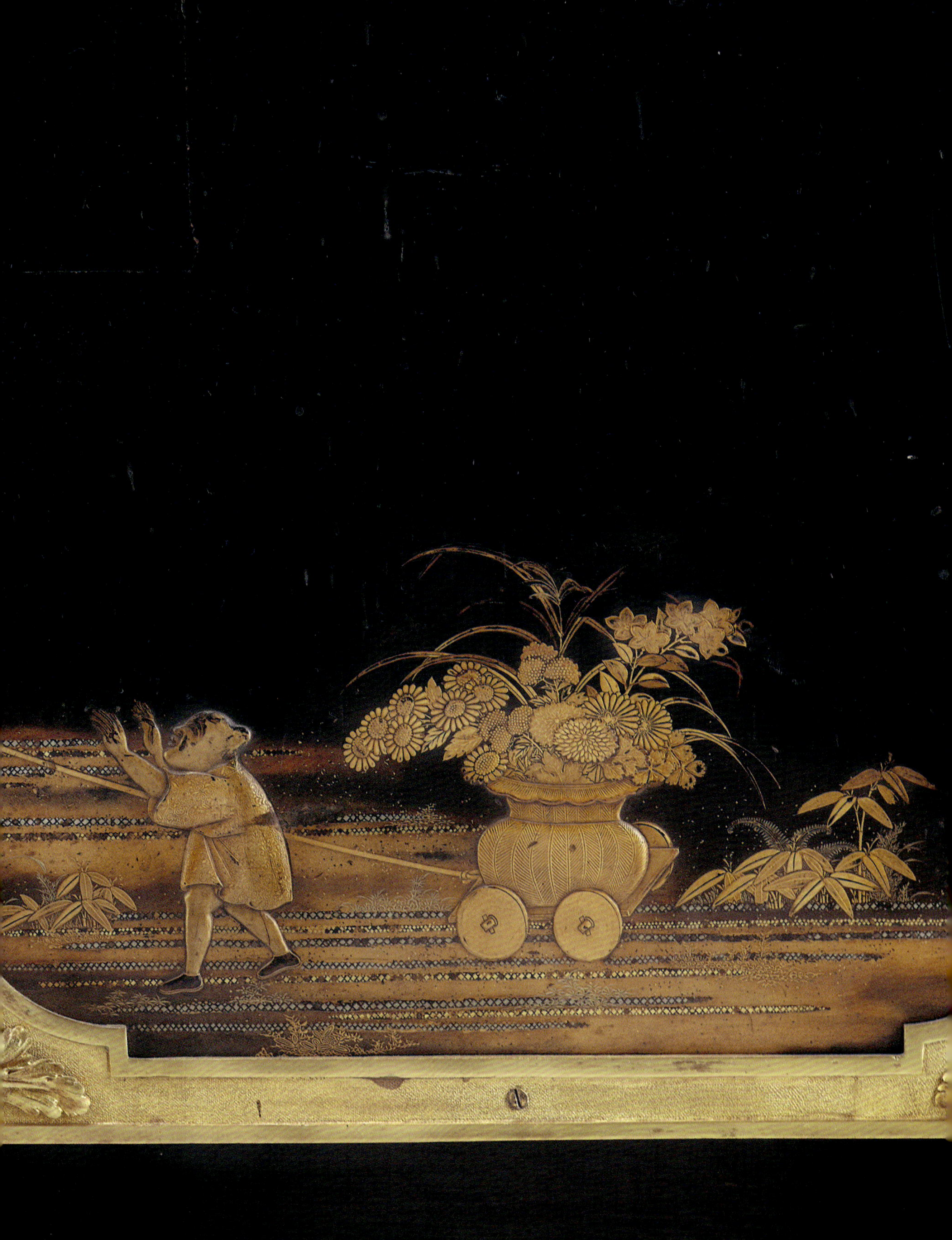

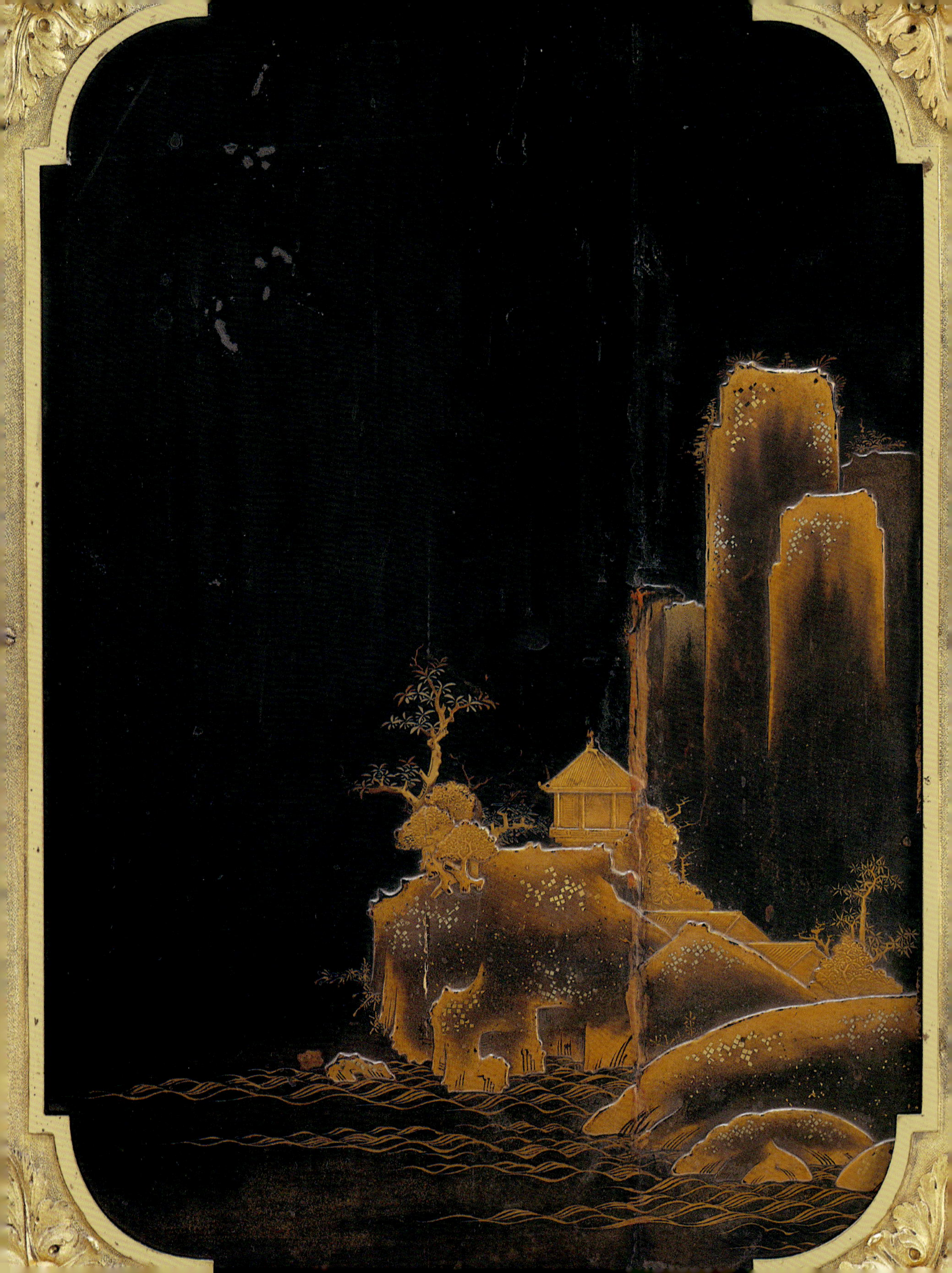

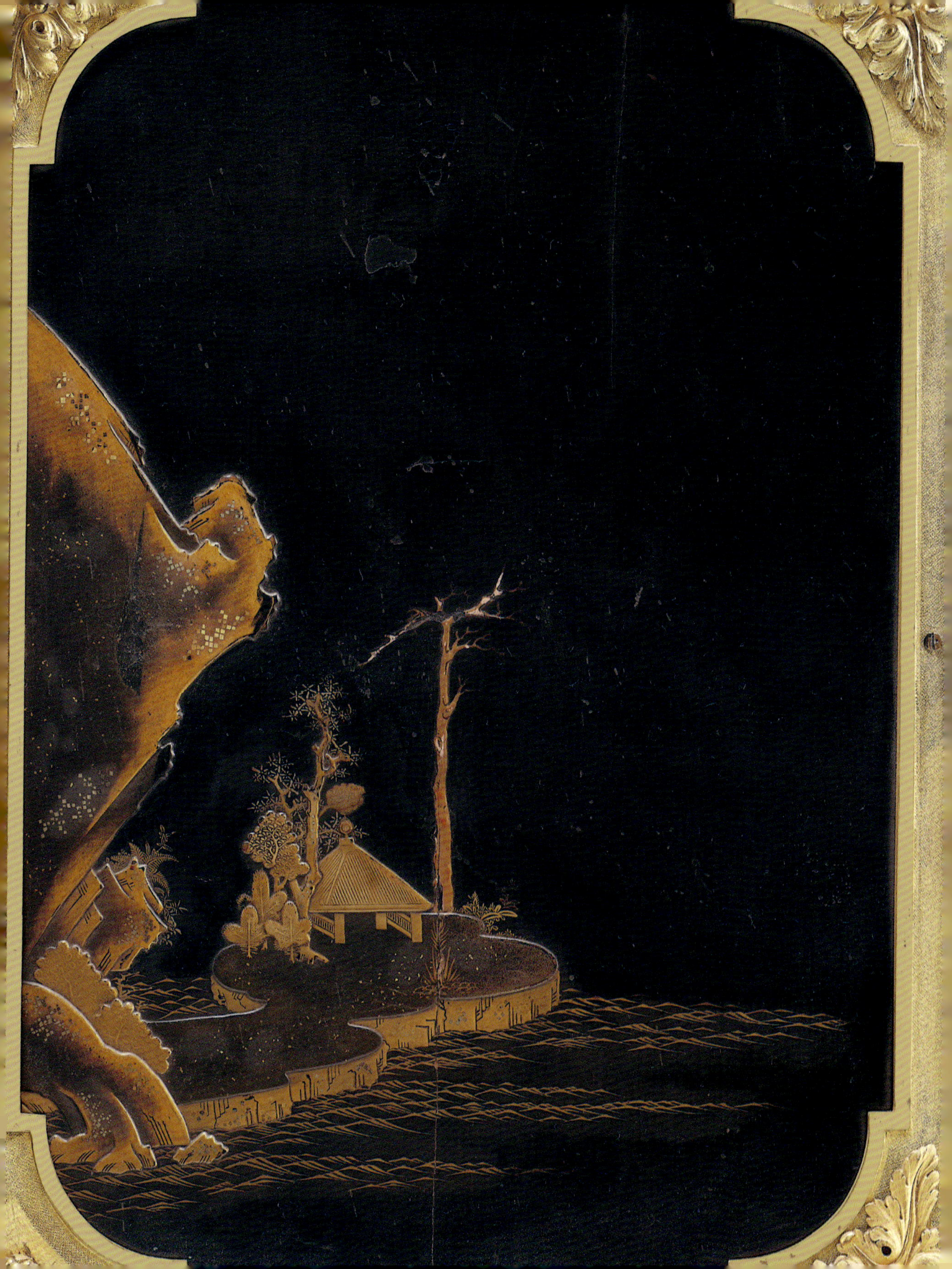

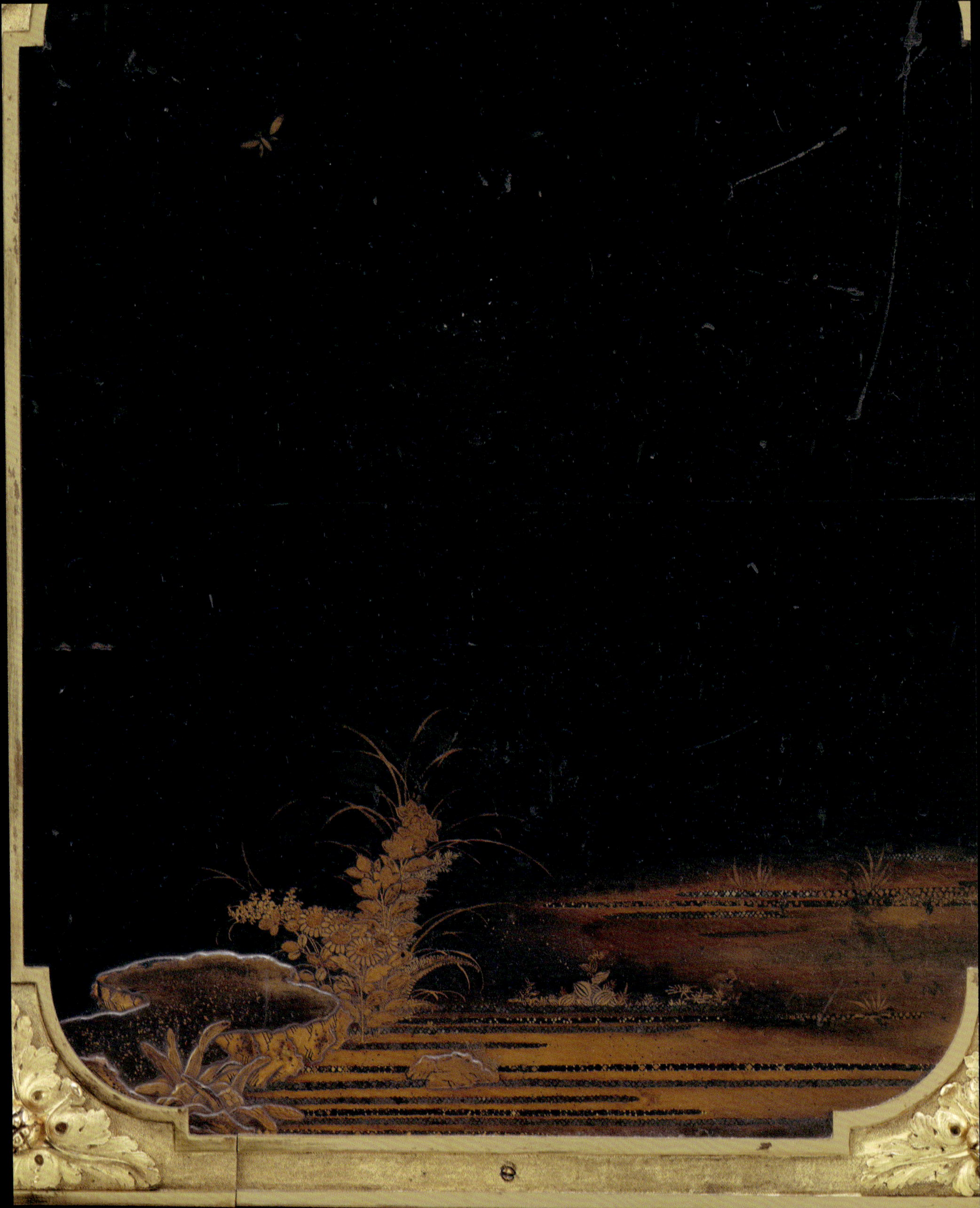

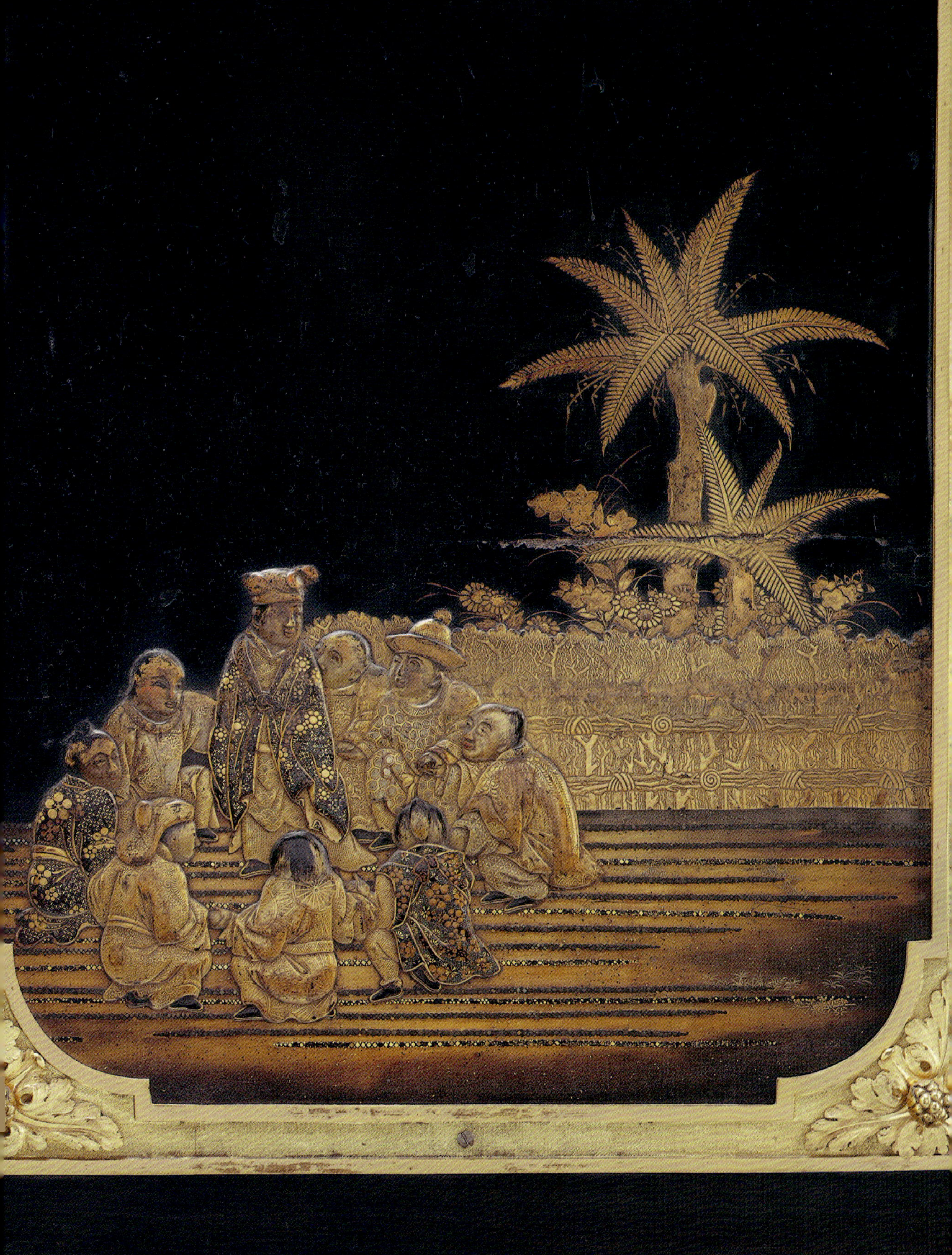

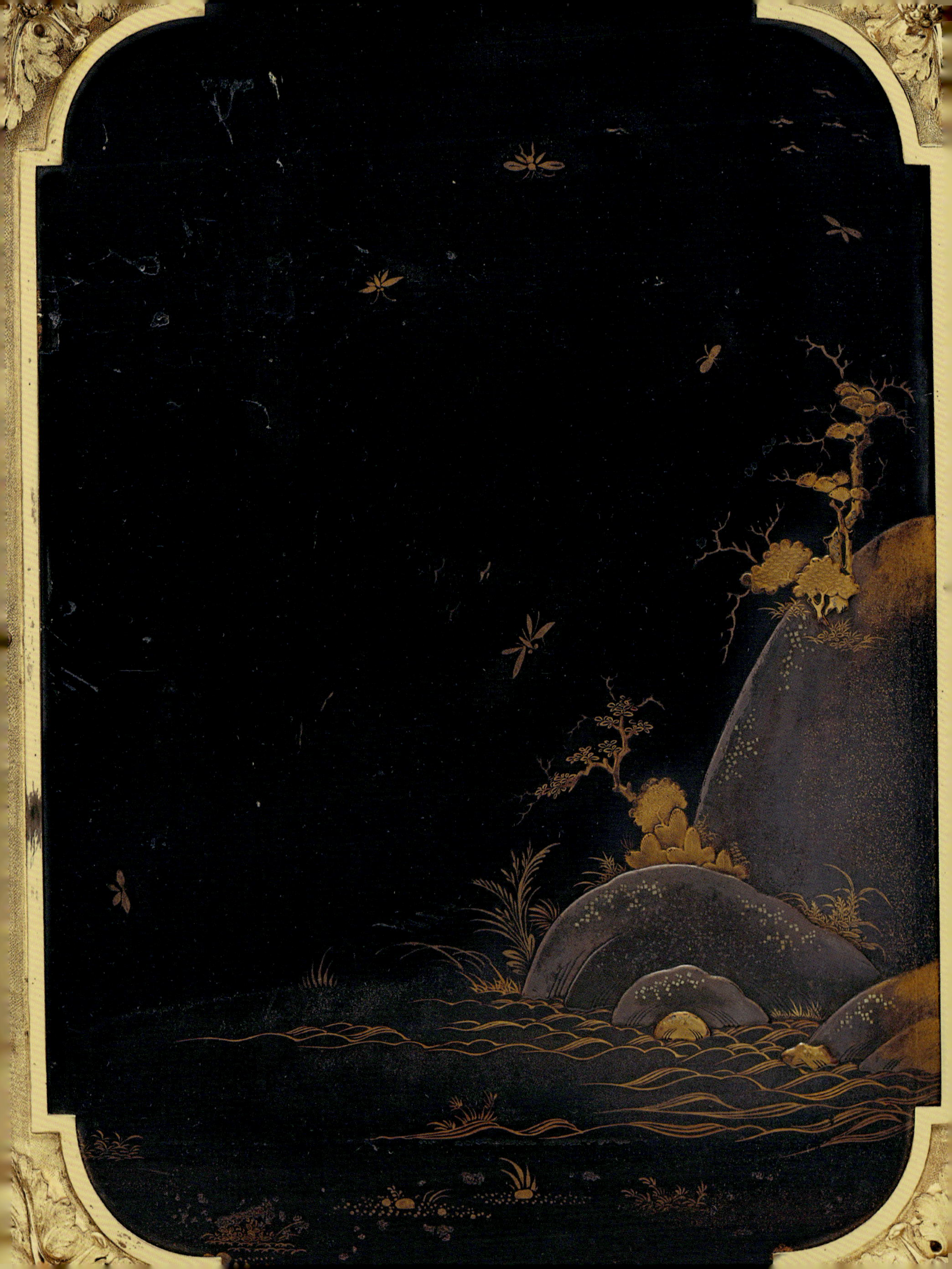

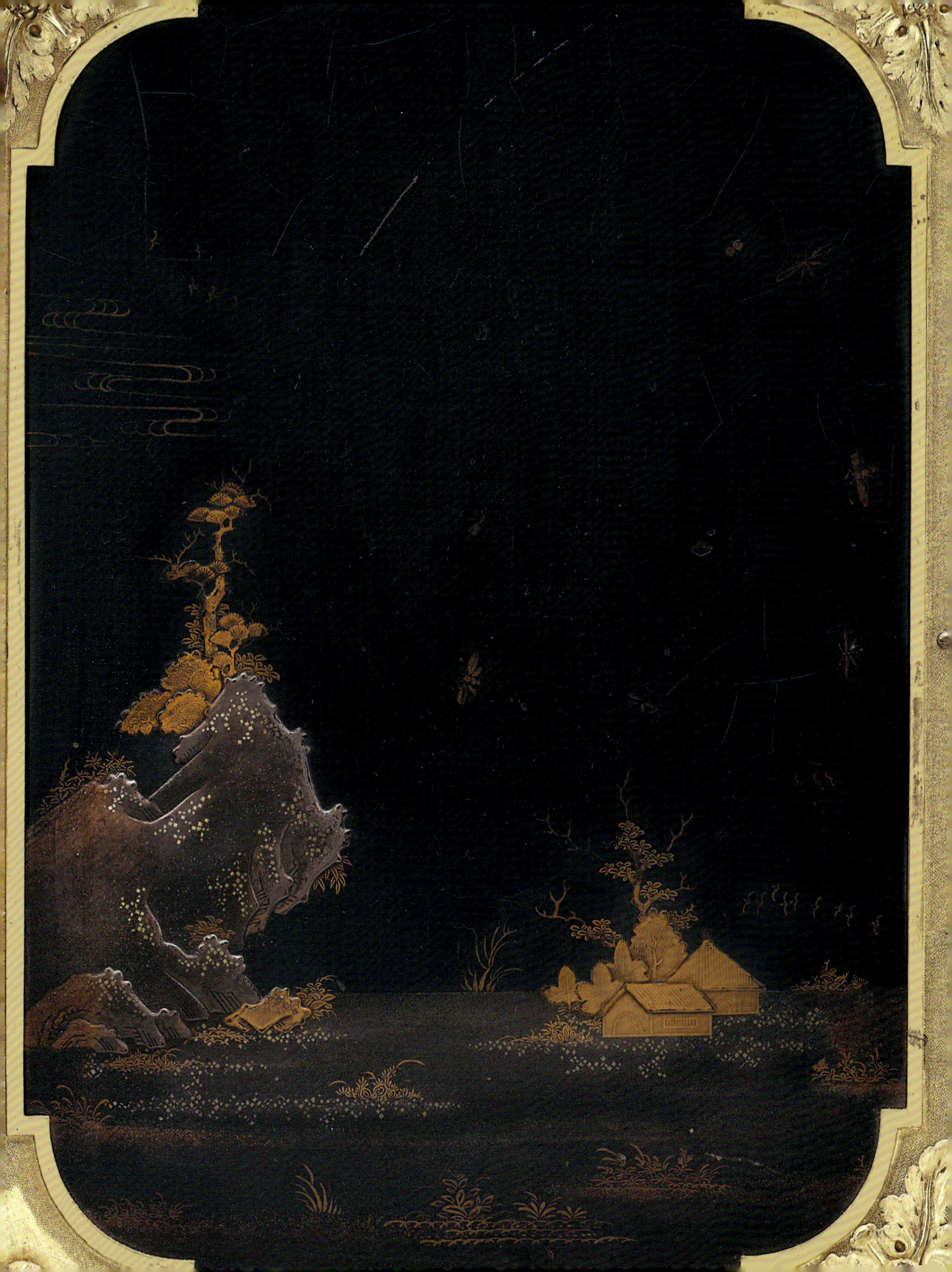

Fig. 8
Bernard van Risenburgh II
Commode, 1745
Oak veneered with panels
of Japanese lacquers, walnut
(drawers), amaranth, nacre,
European varnish, gilt-bronze
mounts, Brèche d'Alep marble
h. 34 in. (89 cm), l. 63 in.
(159 cm), w. 26 ¼ in. (66.5 cm)
Château de Versailles, Versailles

BVRB II and BVRB III, a Dynasty of Talented Cabinetmakers

Born in Paris around 1696 or 1697, Bernard van Risenburgh II—known as BVRB II, though his stamp was always just BVRB—belonged to a family of Dutch cabinetmakers.[16] The first BVRB—who, however, does not seem to have used the four-letter stamp—was quite successful. His *inventaire après-décès* (inventory drawn up after death), compiled on January 7, 1738, indicates that he was relatively well established, with 600 *livres* and silver pieces estimated at 1,433 *livres*.[17] To put that into perspective, an unskilled domestic servant earned about one *livre* a day, an unskilled worker would receive about 220 *livres* a year, and a skilled worker about 500 a year. And in 1768, Voltaire estimated that a person living in Paris needed at least 240 *livres* a year to cover minimum expenses (accommodation, food, and clothes).[18] Likely trained by his father, BVRB II obtained his *maîtrise* (the title received upon successful completion of an apprenticeship in the workshop of a master cabinetmaker followed by several years as a journeyman) around 1730. Before opening a workshop, he

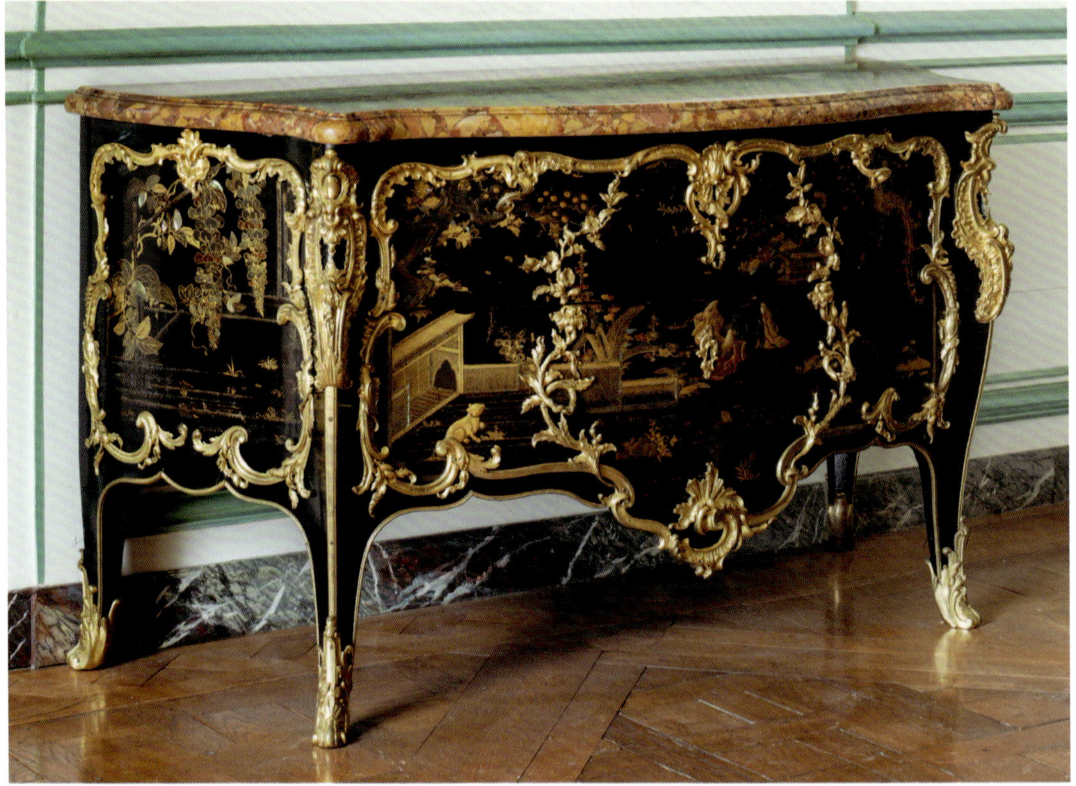

would then have had to prove his competence by making a chef-d'oeuvre or masterpiece. He then established himself on rue de Reuilly in the Faubourg Saint-Antoine, close to his father's workshop, before moving first to the rue Saint-Nicolas, in the Faubourg Saint-Antoine, and then to rue Charenton.[19] He likely traveled to Portugal between 1730 and 1738, where he worked for the king, John V (r. 1706–50), who commissioned works from cabinetmakers, such as Charles Cressent (1685–1768), and Parisian silversmiths.[20] BVRB II and his wife, Geneviève Lavoye, had six children. The dowry given by his father demonstrates that the cabinetmaker started his career comfortably, as he brought 5,000 *livres* to the union.[21]

Beginning in the 1730s, BVRB II worked almost exclusively with several *marchands merciers* (tastemakers and merchants of luxury goods).[22] Other talented cabinetmakers, such as Joseph Baumhauer (d. 1772)—often known simply as Joseph to his contemporaries—Martin Carlin, René Dubois (1737–1799), and Adam Weisweiler (1746–1820), also worked with the most

Fig. 9
Bernard van Risenburgh II
Commode, ca. 1760–65
Oak, fruitwood (?), Japanese lacquer panels, black-japanned veneers, gilt-bronze mounts, black-and-gold Portoro "macchia larga" marble
h. 34 ½ in. (87.5 cm), l. 56 ¾ in. (144 cm), w. 24 ½ in. (62 cm)
Victoria and Albert Museum, London

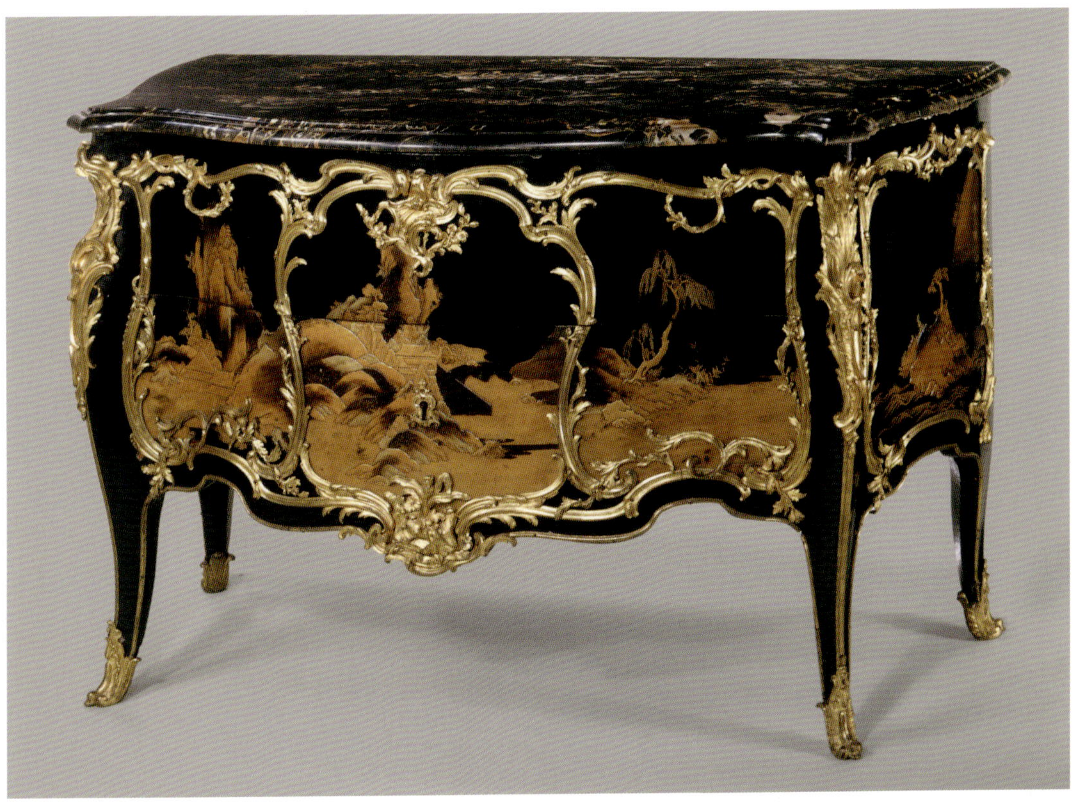

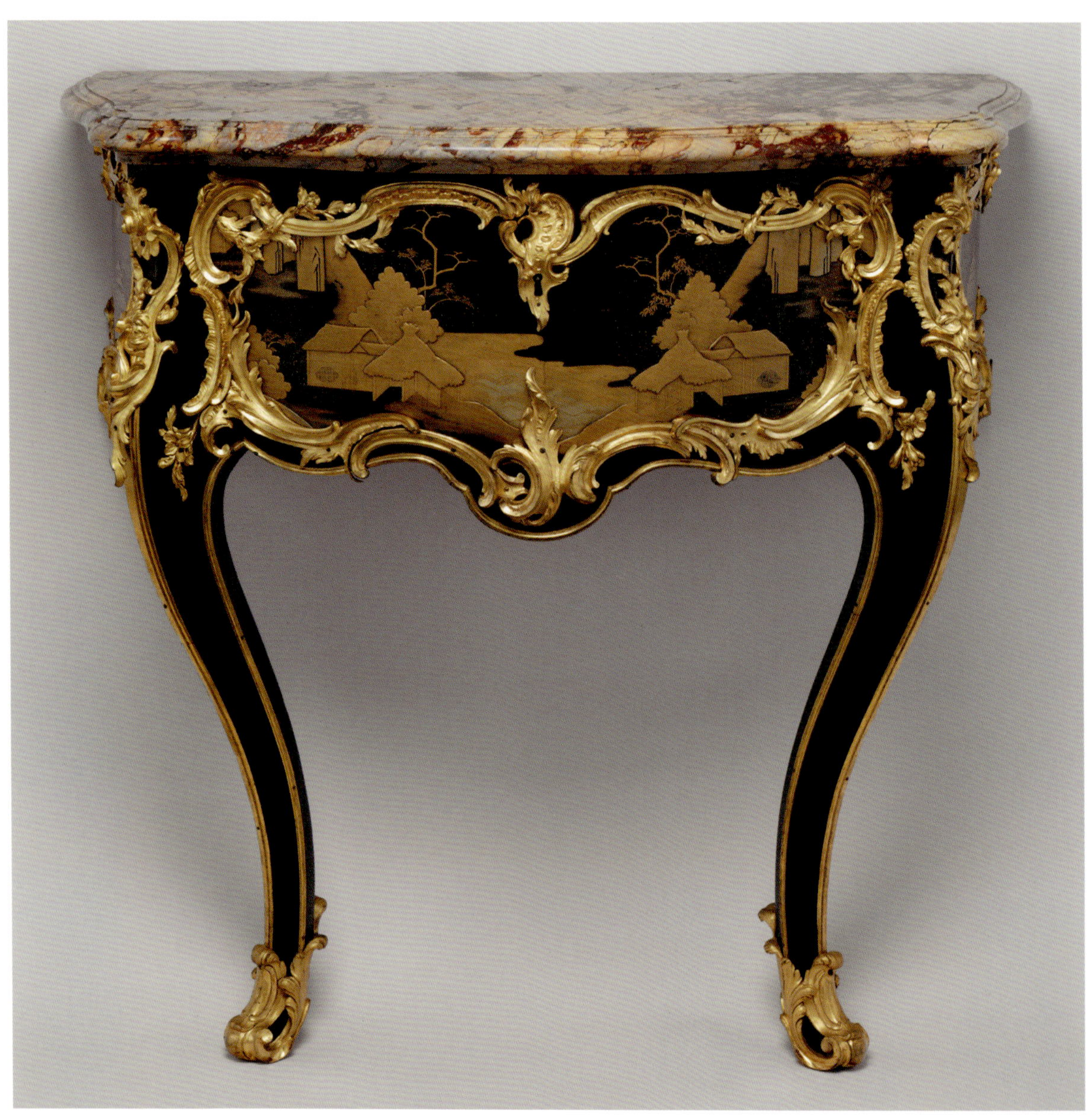

Fig. 10
Bernard van Risenburgh II
Commode en console (Side Table), ca. 1755–60
Oak and pine lacquered black and veneered with Japanese black-
and-gold lacquer, gilt-bronze mounts, Sarrancolin marble top
h. 35½ in. (90.2 cm), l. 37½ in. (95.3 cm), w. 21 in. (53.3 cm)
The Metropolitan Museum of Art, New York

important *marchands merciers* of the eighteenth century. BVRB II's commode with panels of Japanese lacquer, undoubtedly one of his most significant works, was delivered by the *marchand mercier* Thomas-Joachim Hébert (1687–1773) on September 26, 1737, for the queen's *cabinet de retraite* (private cabinet) located between the king's and queen's bedchambers at the Château de Fontainebleau. Additional pieces of furniture resulted from this collaboration: BVRB II also made a commode with Japanese panels for the bedchamber of the dauphine—Maria Teresa Rafaela of Spain (1726–1746)— which Hébert delivered to Versailles on January 23, 1745 (fig. 8). Several examples of furniture attributed to or made by the cabinetmaker with Japanese lacquer can be found in public collections: a commode dated around 1760–65 (fig. 9);[23] the only known example of a commode *en console* (or side table) with Japanese lacquer, made around 1755–60 (fig. 10); a commode made around 1745 at Windsor Castle; a *secrétaire en pente "dos d'âne"* made around 1750–55 (fig. 11); and a pair of *encoignures* made about 1740 (fig. 12).

BVRB II also used what is now known as Coromandel or Bantam lacquer (a Chinese type initially made primarily for export and named after the trading posts in India and Indonesia belonging to the Vereenidge Oostindische

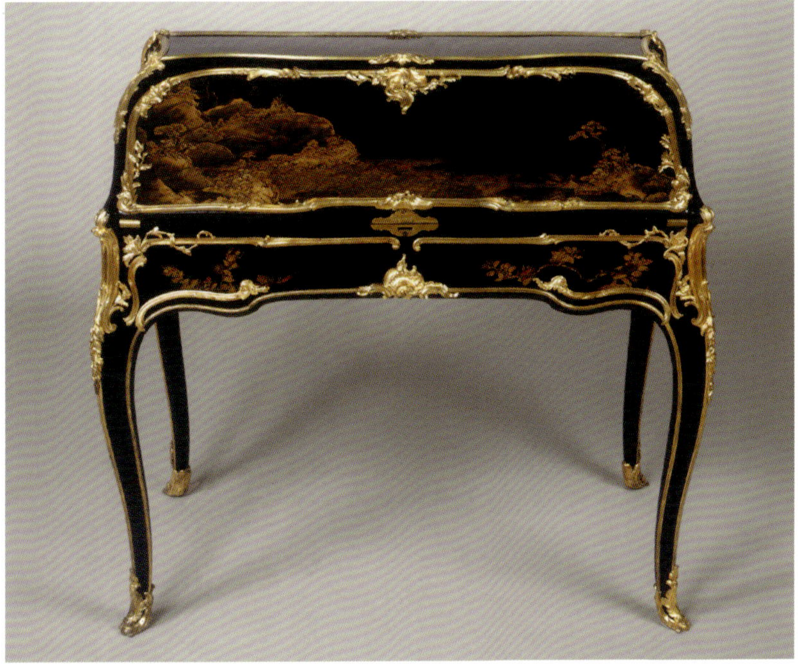

Fig. 11
Attributed to Bernard van Risenburgh II
Secrétaire en pente known as "dos d'âne," ca. 1750–55
Oak, Japanese lacquer, rosewood, violetwood, gilt-bronze mounts
h. 35⅟₁₆ in. (89 cm), l. 36 in. (91.5 cm), w. 18½ in (47 cm)
Waddesdon Manor, Aylesbury, The Rothschild Collection

Compagnie known as the VOC or Dutch East India Company), as seen on a commode attributed to him and made around 1730–35 (fig. 13), a commode of about 1740–45 (fig. 14), and a pair of *encoignures* made around 1745–49 (fig. 15).[24] He also worked with Lazare Duvaux (1703–1758)—Madame de Pompadour's favorite *marchand mercier*—whose sales journal, published by Louis Courajod in 1873, is a valuable source of information about the activities of a *marchand mercier* at the time.[25] Additionally, he collaborated with François-Charles Darnault (ca. 1718–1790) and Simon-Philippe Poirier (1720–1785), who specialized in furniture with lacquer and porcelain plaques. Around 1760, he made a commode for Élisabeth-Thérèse-Alexandrine de Bourbon-Condé (1706–1765), known as Mademoiselle de Sens, that was covered with ninety small porcelain plaques—supported solely by the gilt-bronze nest that surrounds them—likely provided by Poirier, who had access to the Sèvres manufactory (fig. 16).[26]

In October 1764, BVRB II retired, as he was too infirm to continue his work. He sold his workshop—which included his tools—to his son for the relatively small sum of 3,000 *livres*.[27] His stock had about twenty pieces of furniture ready to be veneered, but he did not seem to have any lacquer

Fig. 12
Bernard van Risenburgh II
Pair of Encoignures (Corner Cabinets), ca. 1740
Oak veneered with amaranth, cherrywood, and sycamore maple, set with panels of black Japanese lacquer on Japanese arborvitae, and painted with European lacquer, gilt-bronze mounts, Sarrancolin marble tops
h. 39⅛ in. (99.4 cm), l. 34¾ in. (88.3 cm), w. 24⅛ in. (61.3 cm)
The J. Paul Getty Museum, Los Angeles

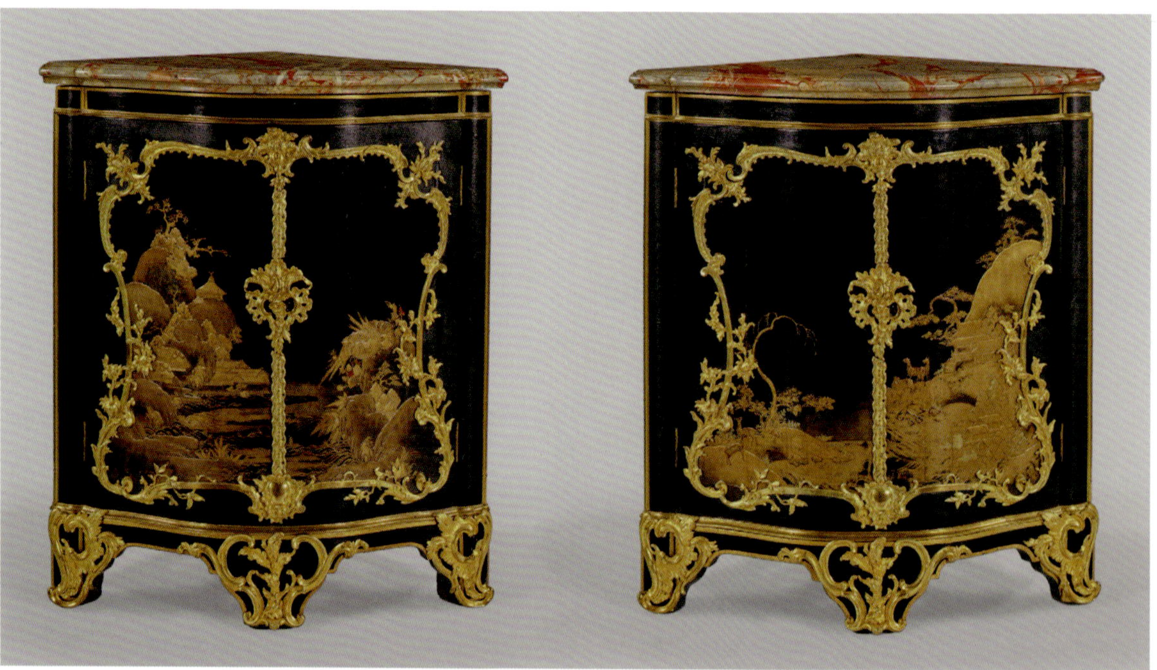

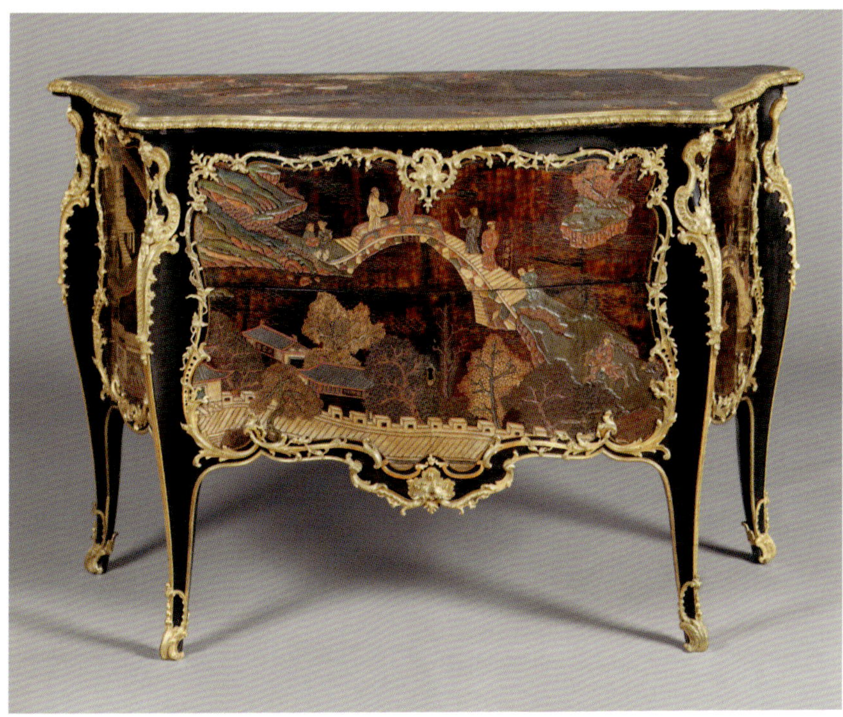

Fig. 13
Attributed to Bernard van
Risenburgh II
Commode, ca. 1730–35
Fir (carcass), oak, walnut
(drawers), Coromandel lacquer,
European varnish, gilt-bronze
mounts
h. 32½ in. (82.5 cm), l. 49⅝ in.
(126 cm), w. 21½ in. (54.5 cm)
Musée du Domaine
Départemental des Hauts-de-
Seine, Sceaux

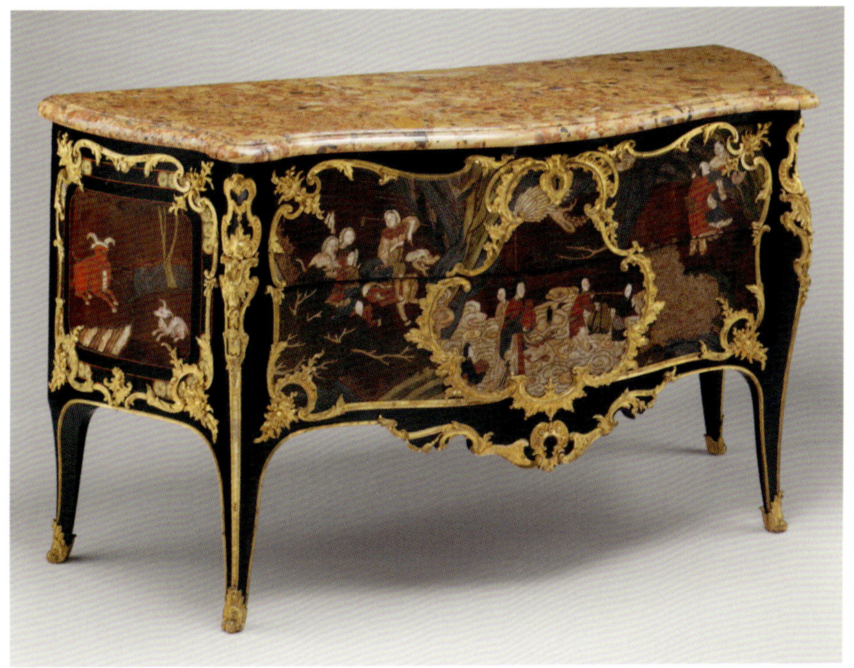

Fig. 14
Bernard van Risenburgh II
Commode, ca. 1740–45
Oak veneered with panels of
Chinese Coromandel lacquer,
European black-lacquered veneer,
gilt-bronze mounts, Brèche
d'Alep marble
h. 34 in. (86.4 cm), l. 63 in.
(160 cm), w. 25¼ in. (64.1 cm)
The Metropolitan Museum of
Art, New York

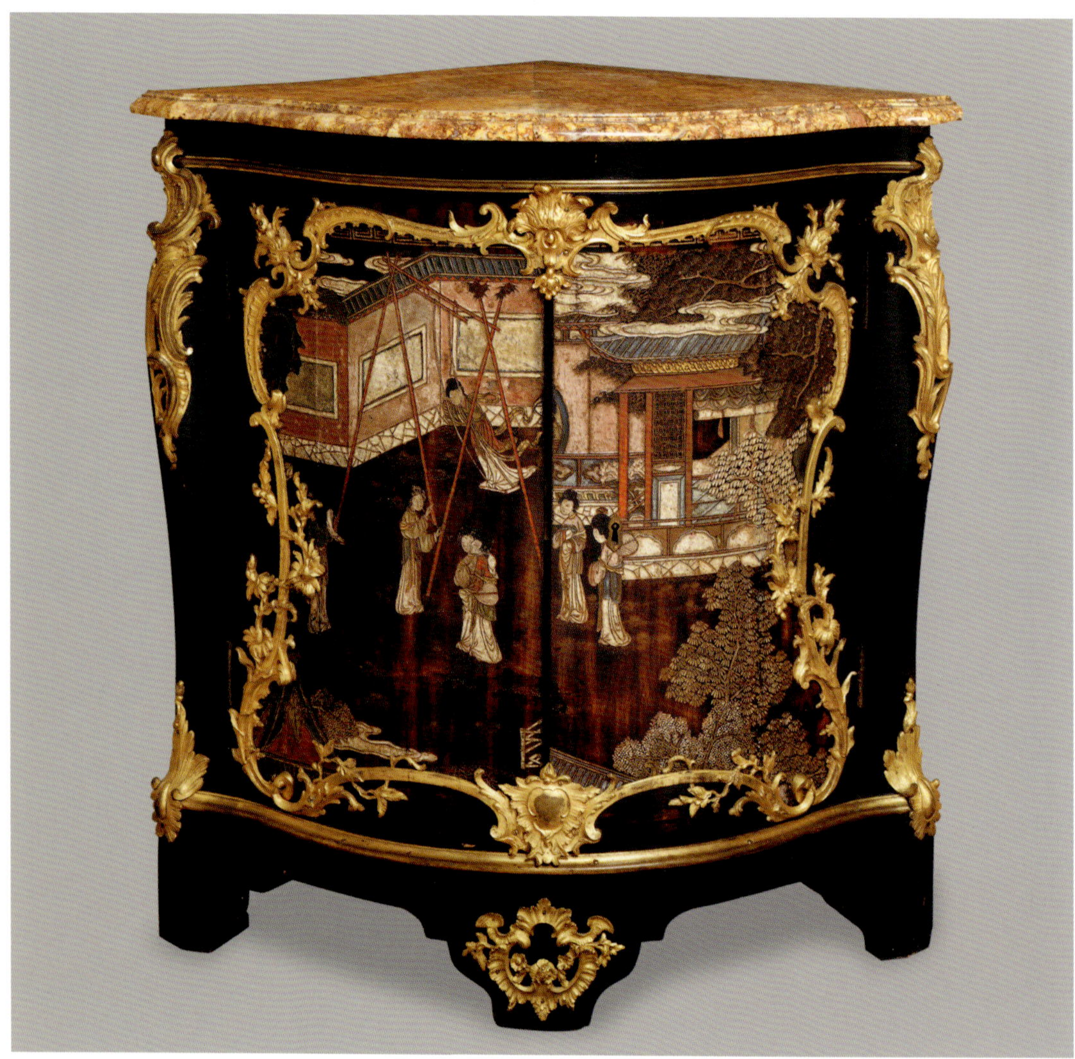

Fig. 15
Bernard van Risenburgh II
Encoignure (one of a pair), ca. 1745–49
Oak veneered with ebony and Coromandel lacquer, cherrywood,
purplewood, gilt-bronze mounts, Brocatelle marble
h. 35⅞ in. (91.1 cm), l. 33⅞ in. (86 cm), w. 26⅛ in. (66.4 cm)
The Metropolitan Museum of Art, New York

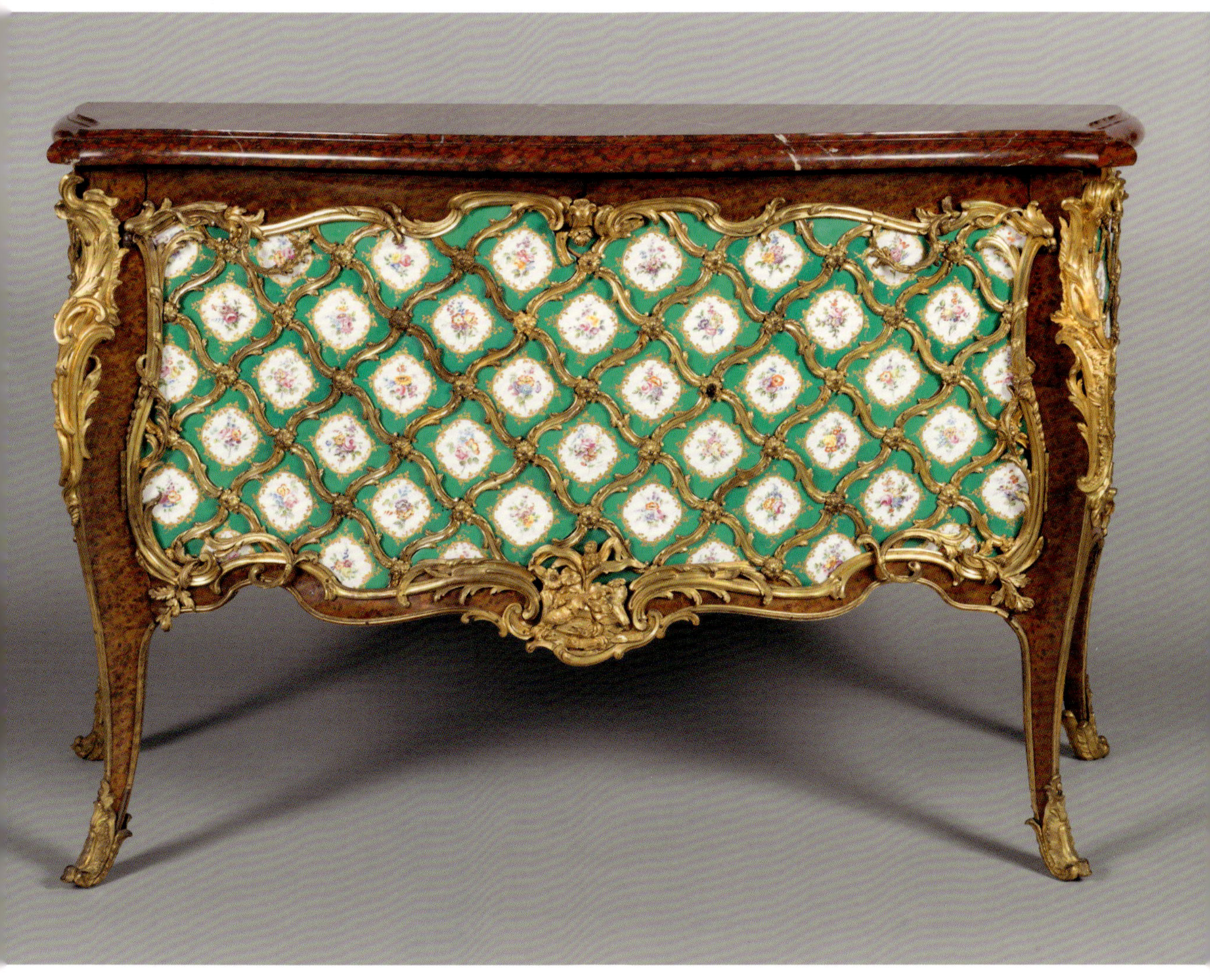

Fig. 16
Bernard van Risenburgh II
Commode, ca. 1760
Rosewood, Sèvres porcelain plaques (1758–60), gilt-bronze
mounts, Griotte marble
h. 35 in. (89 cm), l. 56¼ in. (143 cm), w. 21¼ in. (54 cm)
Private collection

Fig. 17
Bernard van Risenburgh III
Commode, ca. 1765–70
Oak, Japanese black-and-gold
and ebony veneer, gilt-bronze
mounts, Brèche d'Alep marble
h. 36⅛ in. (91.8 cm), l. 64 in.
(162.6 cm), w. 24⅜ in. (61.9 cm)
The Metropolitan Museum of
Art, New York

panels that could have been supplied to him. His financial circumstances were not what one would expect for a cabinetmaker of his caliber. He is but one of numerous remarkable cabinetmakers who worked exclusively with the *marchands merciers* in the hope of remaining financially stable, especially with the associated costs of lacquer panels, but ended their career in a precarious financial position due to their dependence. He likely died before February 1767, as his name does not appear in his son's marriage contract from around that time.[28] Bernard van Risenburgh III was born around 1731–32. He never received his *maîtrise* but as the eldest son followed in his father's footsteps, though with less success, until the death of his mother around 1773–75. Until about 1786, he remained active as a sculptor, providing models for bronzes, an activity his father, who may have designed his own bronzes, also pursued. He died around 1800 without issue, ending the dynasty of cabinetmakers.

In 1957, Jean-Pierre Baroli wrote that, between 1740 and 1775, BVRB II's style evolved as it followed the changing tastes of the times and that the gilt bronzes on the Frick's commodes—especially the feet and the *chutes d'angles* (protective corner bronzes)—retained features reminiscent of the rocaille style, unlike the those on the commodes produced by his son. The style of BVRB III's

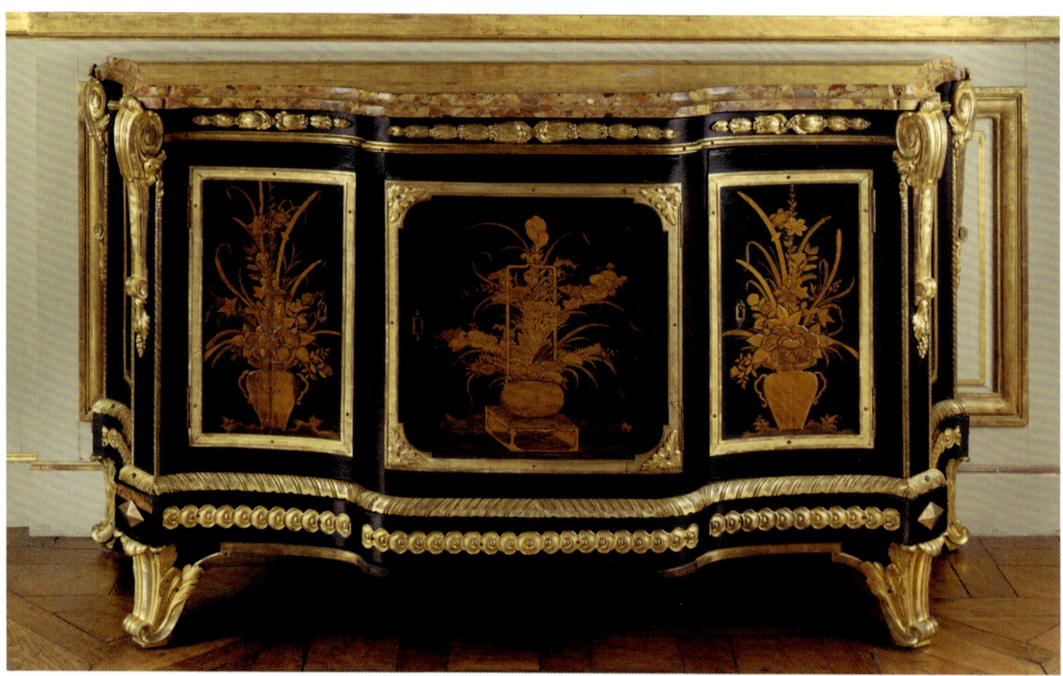

bronzes was more uniform, so much so that Baroli wondered if he did not make them when he was working with his father.[29] More probably, the commodes were begun by BVRB II and completed by his son, who took over the workshop after his father's death.[30] As mentioned above, the inventory prepared after BVRB II's death includes two pieces of furniture in the new style ready to be veneered, evidence that he had started to transition toward the neoclassical style. Two commodes mentioned in the inventory drawn up in 1764 were linked (with no confirmation, though they are the only extant examples that seem to correspond to the description in the archives) to the two examples at the Frick: "Two commodes (carcasses) in the antique style on one of which work was begun to install the doors and side frames and the mouldings (bronzes) at the top and the bottom in copper."[31] It should be noted, however, that several scholars believe that all Van Risenburgh II works produced after 1760 should be reattributed to BVRB III alone. Alexandre Pradère also suggests that the Frick's commodes and other pieces of furniture, including a commode made around 1765–70 (fig. 17), should be attributed to BVRB III. The commode was probably ordered by Poirier, who collaborated with BVRB III before working with Baumhauer, Carlin, and RVLC.[32] Others see links between the neoclassical commode with Japanese lacquer made by Baumhauer and delivered to the marquis de Marigny in 1766 and the production of neoclassical commodes by BVRB III, including the commodes at the Frick.[33] It is difficult to assess what BVRB II's contribution was compared with the work of BVRB III, as his son continued to use his stamp on furniture a few years after his death. BVRB III benefited from his mother's rights, who, as a widow, was entitled to pursue her husband's activity and keep the workshop.

The Popularity of Asian Lacquerware in the Seventeenth and Eighteenth Centuries

The Van Risenburgh commodes are best viewed in the context of the fashion for what we call chinoiserie and turquerie, the eighteenth-century taste for things from China and the Ottoman Empire, respectively.[34] The popularity was an outgrowth of the increased diplomatic relations between Europe and these two regions. In 1721 and 1742, Ottoman embassies were received by Louis XV to renew the association between the two powers. The alliance had been initially established by Francis I (1494–1547) and Suleiman I "the Magnificent" (1494–1566) in 1536 to fight against the Habsburgs, the common enemy of

Following pages:

Fig. 18
Filippo Juvarra and Benedetto Alfieri
The Chinese Cabinet,
ca. 1732–36
Palazzo Reale, Turin

Fig. 19
Panel from the Lacquer Room in the Hôtel du Châtelet built by Mathurin Cherpitel for Count Florent du Châtelet, ca. 1770–71 (for the room)
Carcass of oak, Chinese lacquer panel with red ground and black-and-gold decoration, amaranth frame, painting in imitation of tulipwood
Musée des Arts Décoratifs, Paris (long-term loan from the Ministère du Travail)

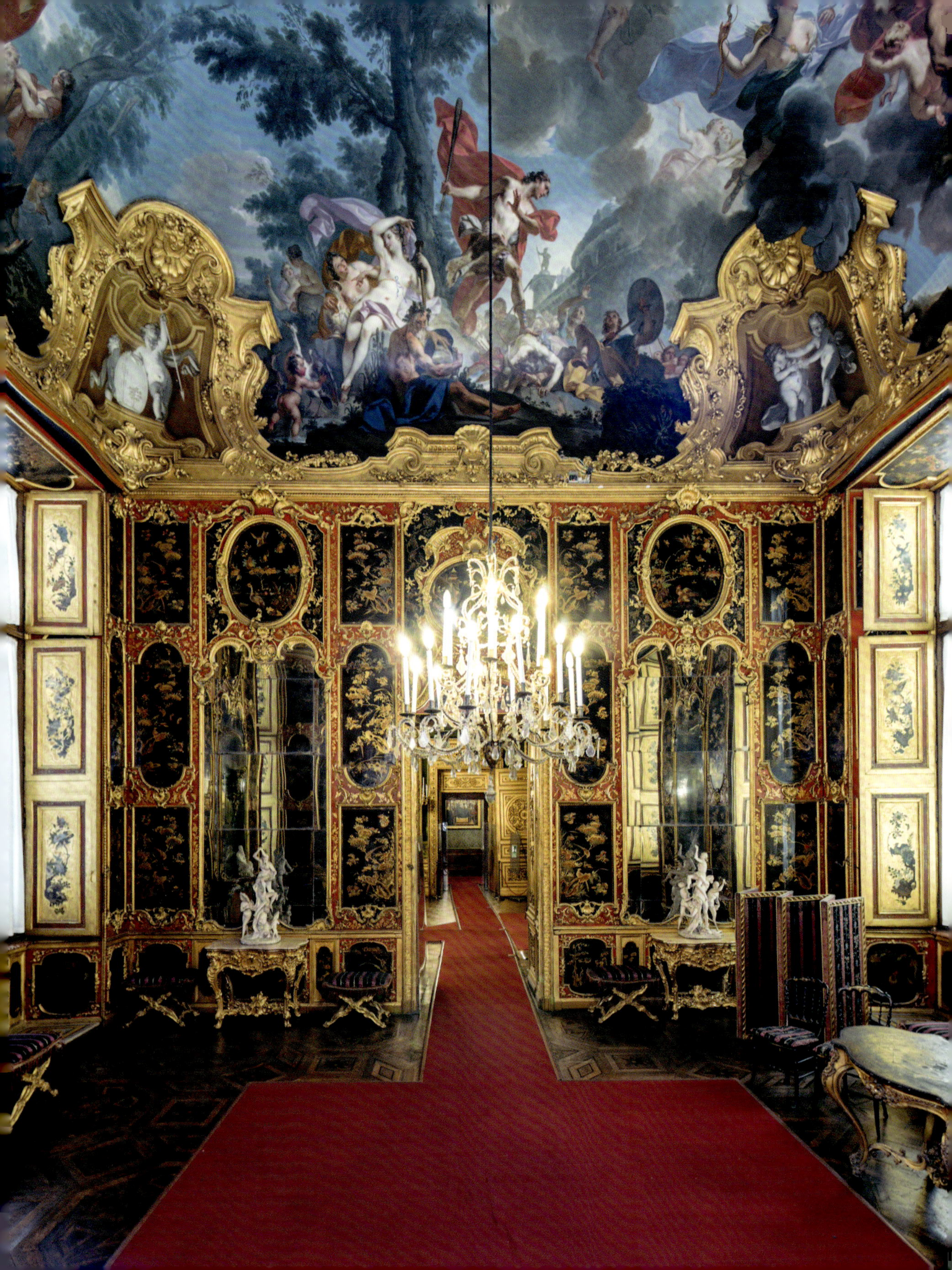

both empires. Notably, diplomatic relations between France and China were established under the reign of Louis XIV (r. 1643–1715).[35] From porcelain and furniture to small rooms covered entirely with Asian (predominantly Chinese) lacquerware (figs. 18 and 19), turqueries and chinoiseries remained Western interpretations of Eastern themes, although accounts from Jesuits established in Asia in the seventeenth and the eighteenth centuries slowly reached France and provided a more accurate description of regions outside Europe.

A resin made from the sap of trees in the sumac family (especially *Rhus vernicifera* or *verniciflua)* and found in various parts of Asia (especially China, Japan, and Korea), lacquer was made available to Europe by the Portuguese, who established trade in China during the sixteenth century.[36] With the creation of the VOC in 1602 and the Compagnie des Indes—its French counterpart founded in 1664 by Louis XIV—France finally had access to the market.[37] Initially, objects fabricated with lacquer were extremely expensive, as they were the product of a lengthy technical process. Whereas the secret to making porcelain "in the Chinese manner" in Europe was not discovered until the eighteenth century, the process for making lacquer had already been described by Portuguese Jesuits in China at the end of the sixteenth and the early part of the seventeenth centuries. (The technique had been known in Asia since antiquity.[38])

The traditional process for making lacquer begins with tapping the trees for sap between the months of June and December (fig. 20a–c). The sap then drips until it is harvested, usually between June and July. Once collected, the sap is refined through a lengthy filtering process, after which the lacquer is colored with one or more of a very few pigments: black made of bone char, red from cinnabar, yellow from orpiment, green from a mix of orpiment and indigo, brown from iron oxide, and white from lead white and oil. Using brushes made of animal hair, the artisan applies the lacquer in thin coats, in a hot and humid space but not far from a window to let the lacquer dry.[39] Several

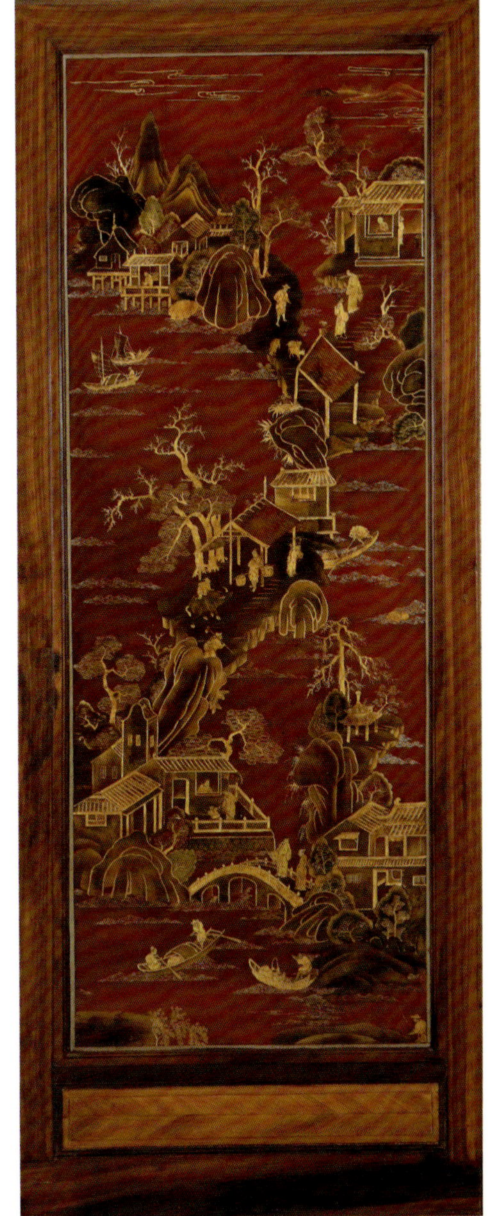

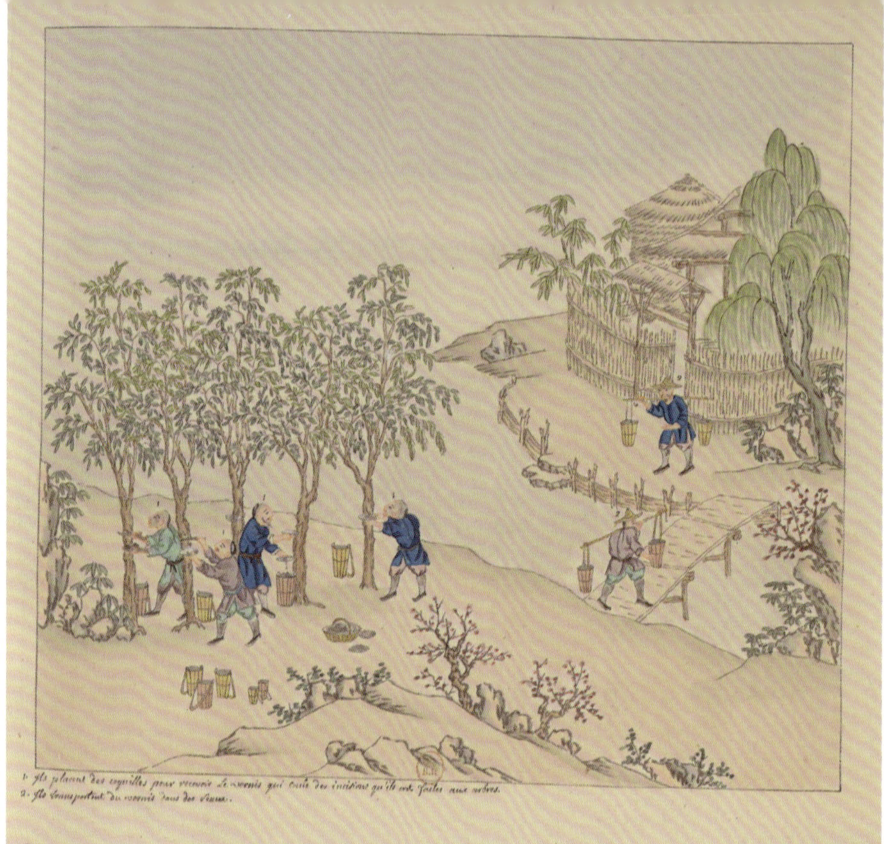

Fig. 20a–c
Steps illustrating the making of lacquers from an album of engravings *[Art de recueillir, de préparer et d'appliquer le vernis à la Chine]*, 18th century
Chinese black ink, Chinese colored ink
Bibliothèque Nationale de France, Paris

coats—with two days of drying and polishing between each application—are required to build a thickness of one-sixteenth of an inch.

As demand increased, Japanese and Chinese artisans began to produce lacquerware for export, though this was generally of lower quality. They also started to adapt their production to the taste of their clients, providing sought-after objects such as small boxes, *cabarets* (trays with cups and other pieces for serving tea and coffee), and screens. The center of high-quality lacquerware in the eighteenth century was in Japan, with most craftsmen—whether they worked for the imperial court or foreign merchants—established in Kyoto. Lacquerware also reached Europe through diplomatic channels via the custom of gift exchanges among monarchs. Stéphane Castelluccio has noted that European courts sometimes relied on embassies to provide lacquerware. In September 1686, an embassy from Phra Narai (1632–1688), King of Siam, offered Louis XIV and several members of the royal family, such as the Grand Dauphin, numerous gifts with lacquers (fig. 21).[40] Among those for the king were twenty-three cabinets, at least three of which were made in "Meaco" (former appellation for Kyoto), the producer of the most expensive and rare lacquerware of the time.[41] Most of the other gifts made of lacquer were also

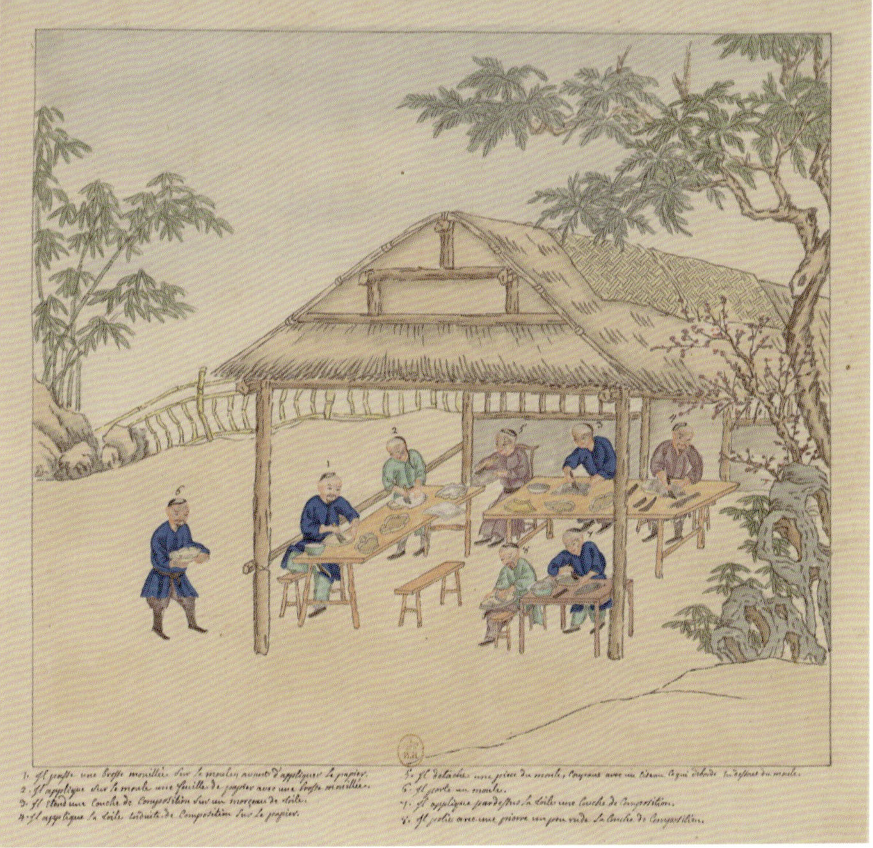

1. Il passe une brosse mouillée sur le moule avant d'appliquer le papier.
2. Il applique sur le moule une feuille de papier avec une brosse mouillée.
3. Il étend une couche de Composition sur un morceau de toile.
4. Il applique la toile enduite de Composition sur le papier.
5. Il détache une pièce du moule, l'ouvrant avec un ciseau ce qui déborde au dessus du moule.
6. Il porte au moule.
7. Il applique par dessus la toile une couche de Composition.
8. Il polit avec une pierre un peu rude la couche de Composition.

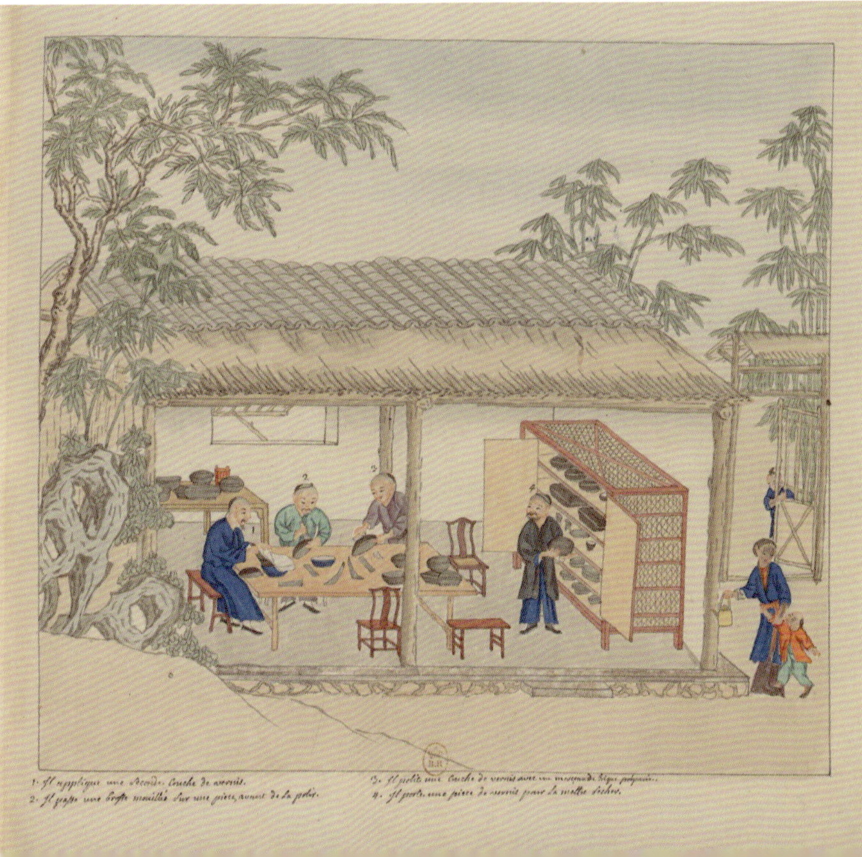

1. Il applique une seconde couche de vernis.
2. Il passe une brosse mouillée sur une pièce, avant de la polir.
3. Il polit une couche de vernis avec un morceau de bigne préparé.
4. Il porte une pièce de vernis pour la mettre sécher.

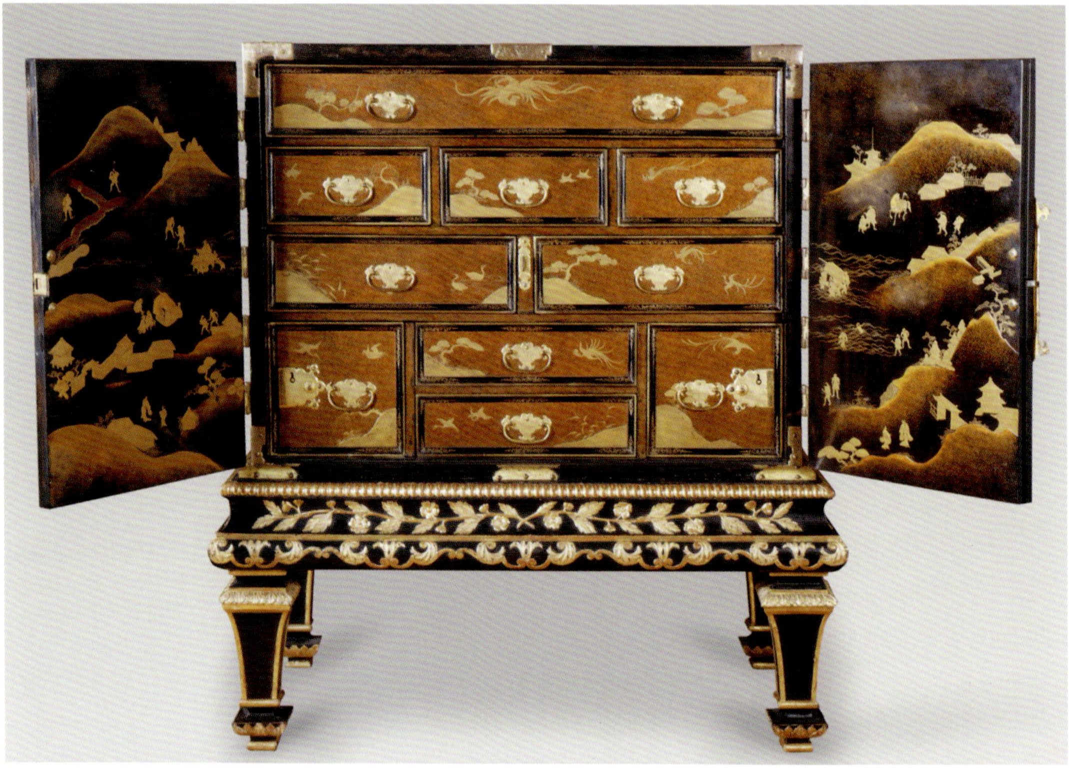

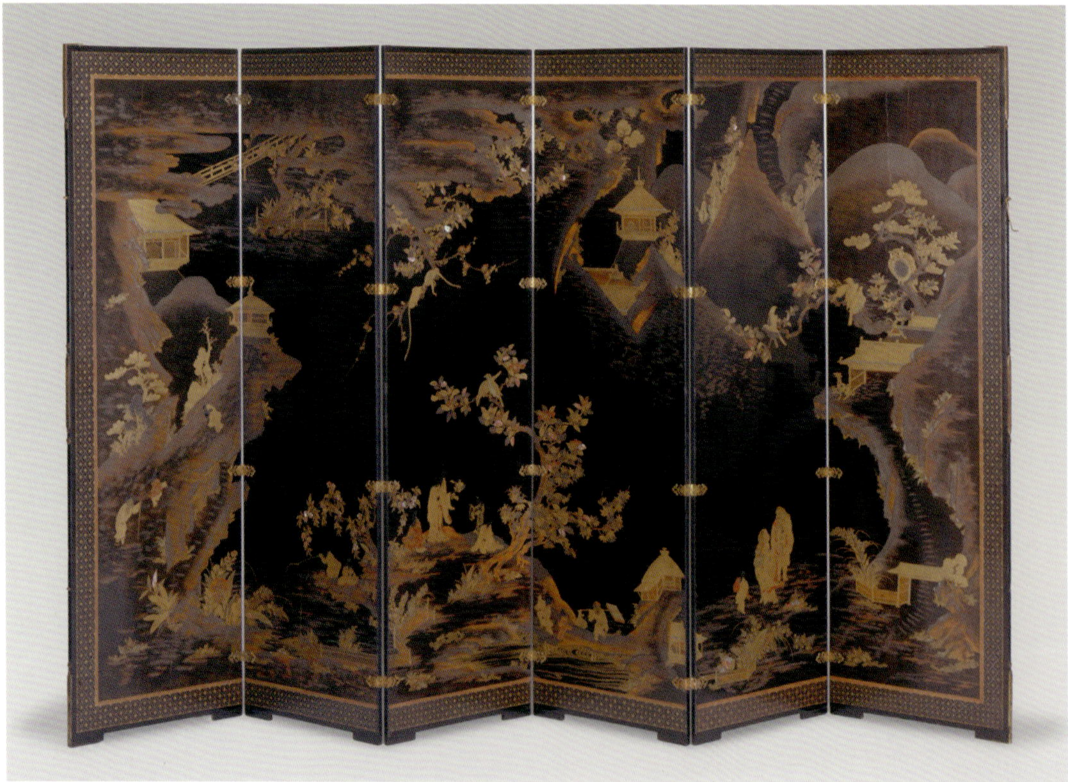

from Japan. Among these were about fifty boxes and small chests and three screens, which, because of their rarity and value, the royal family kept in the Garde-Meuble de la Couronne.[42]

Among the objects kept at the Garde-Meuble were six Japanese lacquered screens—which were extremely rare in Europe—that had been listed in the 1729 inventory of objects owned by the Crown.[43] These were probably similar to one in the Victoria and Albert Museum, London, the only fully lacquered Japanese screen preserved in a public collection in Europe (fig. 22). When Japan closed its borders to almost all European trade in the seventeenth century (during the Edo period, 1603–1868), other centers of production became privileged: Thailand, where it was still possible to acquire Japanese and Chinese lacquerware, and the coast of India, where merchants could acquire Coromandel lacquerware, which was also used on furniture (fig. 23).[44] Nonetheless, prices for Japanese lacquer were exorbitant in the eighteenth century. Acquiring lacquer pieces on the secondary market after the death of a collector was also a viable option. Finally, it was possible to buy lacquerware from other *marchands merciers* and at the sales organized by the Garde-Meuble.[45]

Fig. 21
Japanese Cabinet (one of a pair), late 17th century
Makie lacquer, gold copper alloy
h. 45¾ in. (116 cm), l. 42⁵⁄₁₆ in. (107.5 cm), w. 24½ in. (62 cm)
Musée du Louvre, Paris

Fig. 22
Six-Paneled Screen, ca. 1660–80
Wood covered in black lacquer, gold, silver and red *hiramakie* lacquer, metal foil, studs, shells
h. 67⁹⁄₁₆ in. (171.6 cm), l. 125 in. (317.5 cm)
Victoria and Albert Museum, London

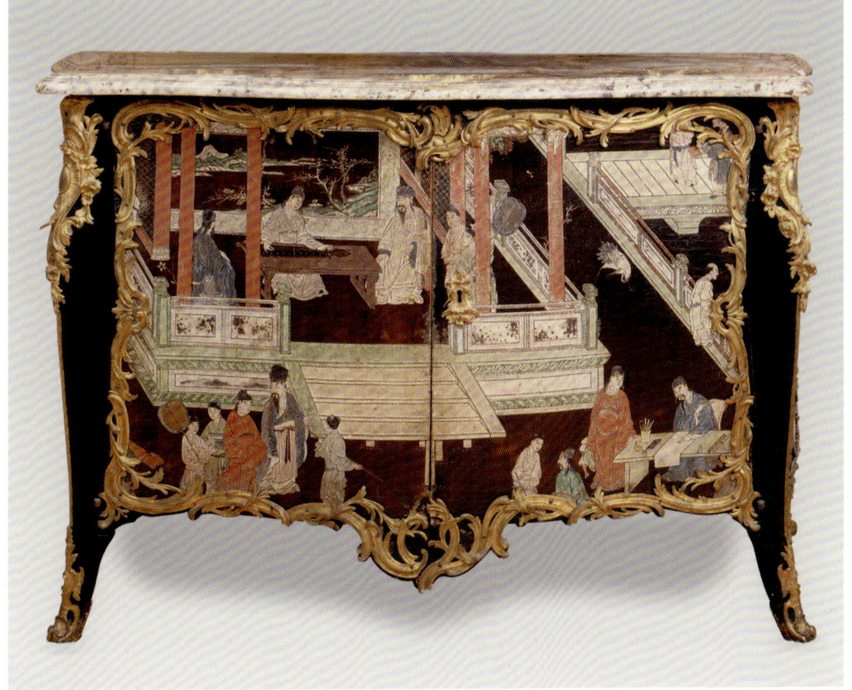

Fig. 23
Jacques-Philippe Carel
Commode, ca. 1750
Black varnished wood, fruitwood, oak, Coromandel lacquer, Sarrancolin marble
h. 36⅞ in. (93.6 cm), l. 58¹⁄₁₆ in. (147.5 cm), w. 27¼ in. (69 cm)
Musée du Louvre, Paris

The *Marchands Merciers*

The important role of the *marchands merciers* is celebrated by Jean-Antoine Watteau (1684–1721) in his painting of the shop of his friend Edme-François Gersaint, *L'Enseigne de Gersaint* (Gersaint's Shop Sign) (fig. 24). Denis Diderot described the *marchand mercier* as a "marchand de tout & faiseur de rien" (seller of everything, maker of nothing) in his *Encyclopédie*, but they were, however, essential to the use of lacquer on furniture, as they supplied most

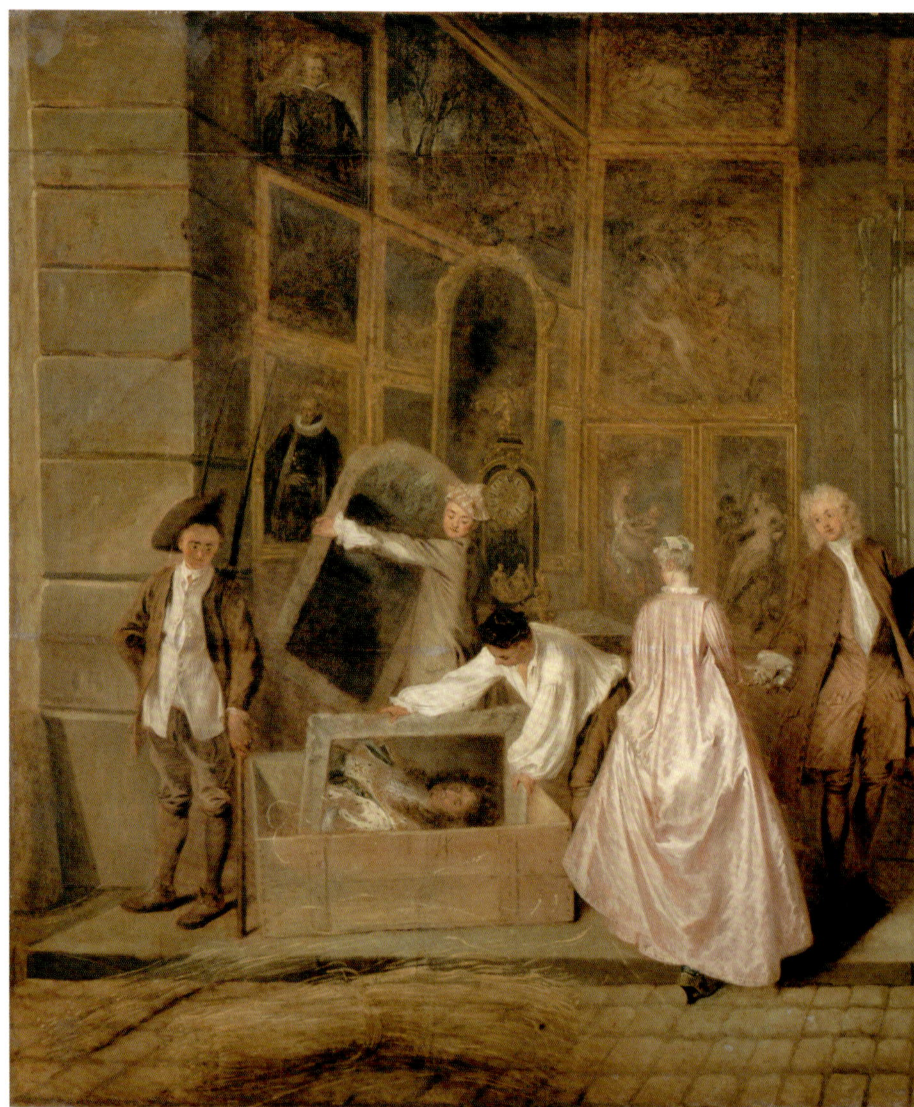

Fig. 24
Jean-Antoine Watteau
L'Enseigne de Gersaint, ca. 1720–21
Oil on canvas
64 ¼ × 121 ¼ in. (163 × 308 cm)
Charlottenburg Palace, Berlin

cabinetmakers in the eighteenth century.[46] The guild created by Charles VI in 1407—the Corporation des Marchands Merciers—was extremely powerful and had the exclusive right to buy and sell lacquerware, although the guild forbade its members to manufacture anything themselves. A trade card designed by François Boucher in 1740 (fig. 25) describes Gersaint's shop—named À la pagode (At the pagoda)—as selling Asian objects, including cabinets with lacquer he could obtain thanks to his multiple trips to Holland:[47]

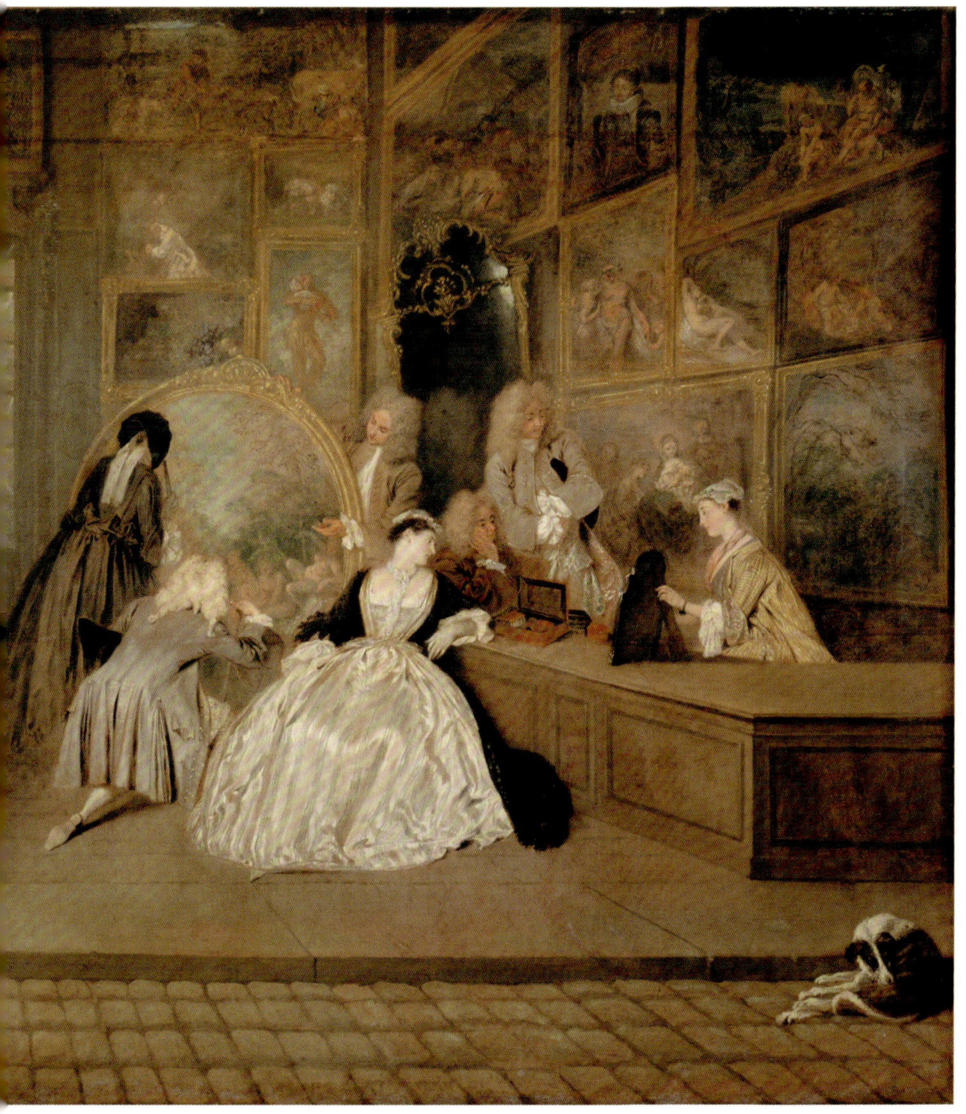

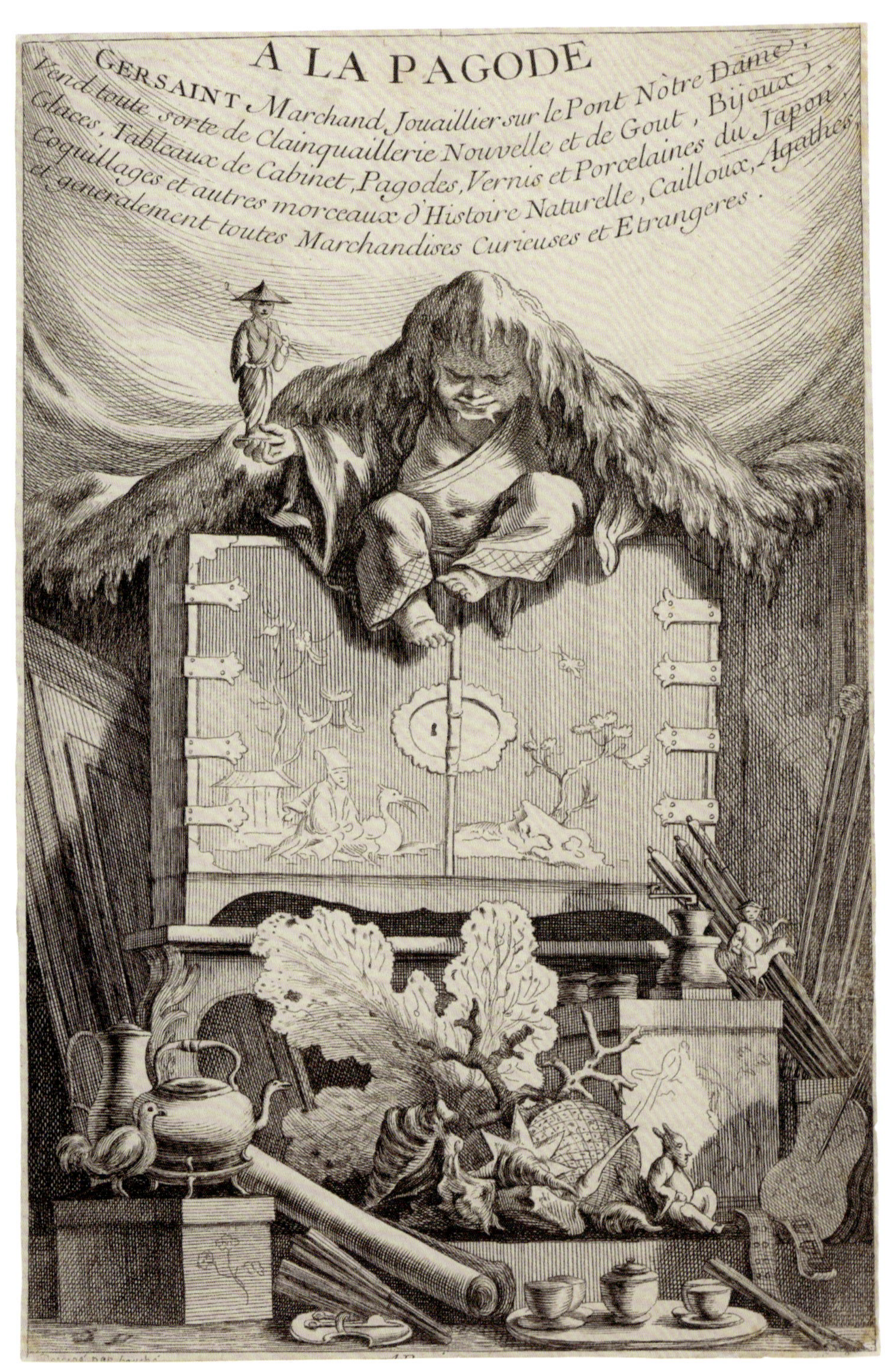

A LA PAGODE
GERSAINT, Marchand, Jouaillier sur le Pont Nôtre Dame,
Vend toute sorte de Clainquaillerie Nouvelle et de Gout, Bijoux,
Glaces, Tableaux de Cabinet, Pagodes, Vernis et Porcelaines du Japon,
Coquillages et autres morceaux d'Histoire Naturelle, Cailloux, Agathes,
et generalement toutes Marchandises Curieuses et Etrangeres.

Gersaint Merchant Jeweler located at the Pont Nôtre Dame sells all kinds of new and tasteful Hardware, Jewelry, Mirrors, Cabinet Paintings, Pagodas, Varnishes and Japanese Porcelain, Shells and other pieces of Natural History, Pebbles, Agates, and generally all kinds of Curious and Foreign Goods.[48]

The *marchands merciers* were established near the Louvre during the seventeenth century, and in the following century relocated to the Right Bank—specifically to the rue Saint-Honoré—where they were closer to their clientele of aristocrats and the powerful *fermiers-généraux* who made their fortunes lending money to the monarchy.[49] The *marchands merciers* decided to dismantle and cut down precious Asian lacquer used to decorate screens, chests, and cabinets so they could provide the panels to cabinetmakers for reuse on furniture. In 1744, for example, the *marchand* Thomas-Joachim Hébert supplied Japanese lacquer panels from a six-leaf screen he received in January from the Garde-Meuble to the cabinetmaker Antoine-Robert Gaudreaus (ca. 1680–1746), who incorporated them into a commode with two drawers for the bedchamber of Louis XV at the Château de Choisy (fig. 26).[50] The screen may have been among those gifted by the king of Siam to Louis XIV in 1686

Fig. 25
Anne Claude Philippe de Tubières, comte de Caylus, after François Boucher
À la pagode (trade card of Edme-François Gersaint), 1740
Etching and engraving
11¼ × 7 ½ in. (28.2 × 18.9 cm)
The Metropolitan Museum of Art, New York

Fig. 26
Antoine-Robert Gaudreaus
Commode, 1744
Oak, walnut, cherrywood, rosewood, Japanese lacquer, European varnish, gilt-bronze mounts, Rance marble
h. 33 ¹⁄₁₆ in. (84 cm), l. 71¼ in. (181 cm), w. 27 ¼ in. (69 cm)
Château de Versailles, Versailles

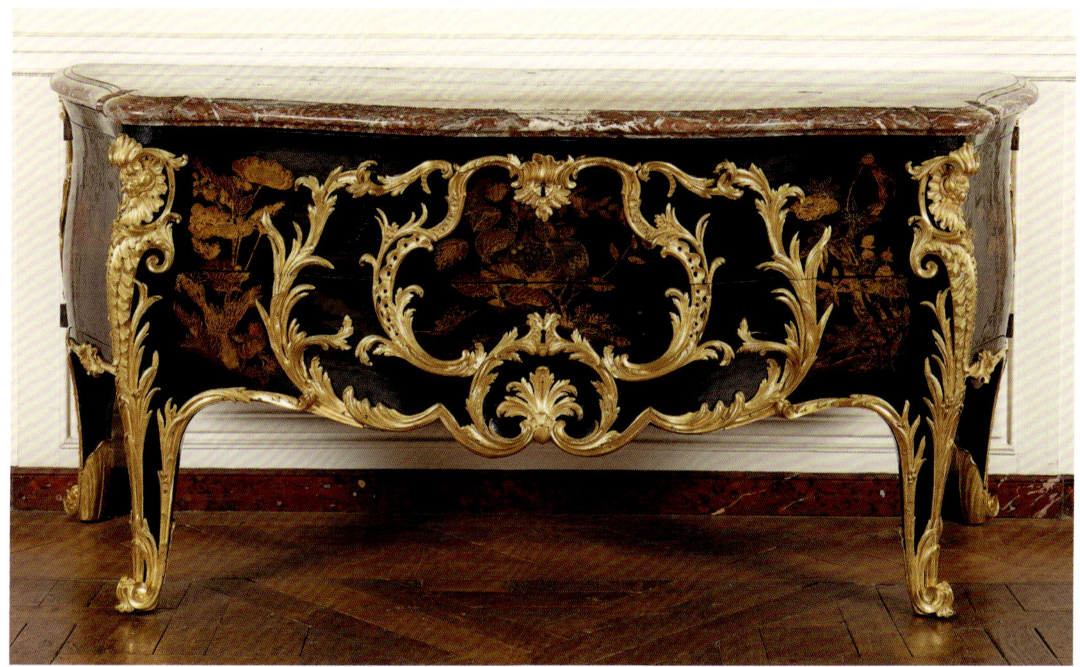

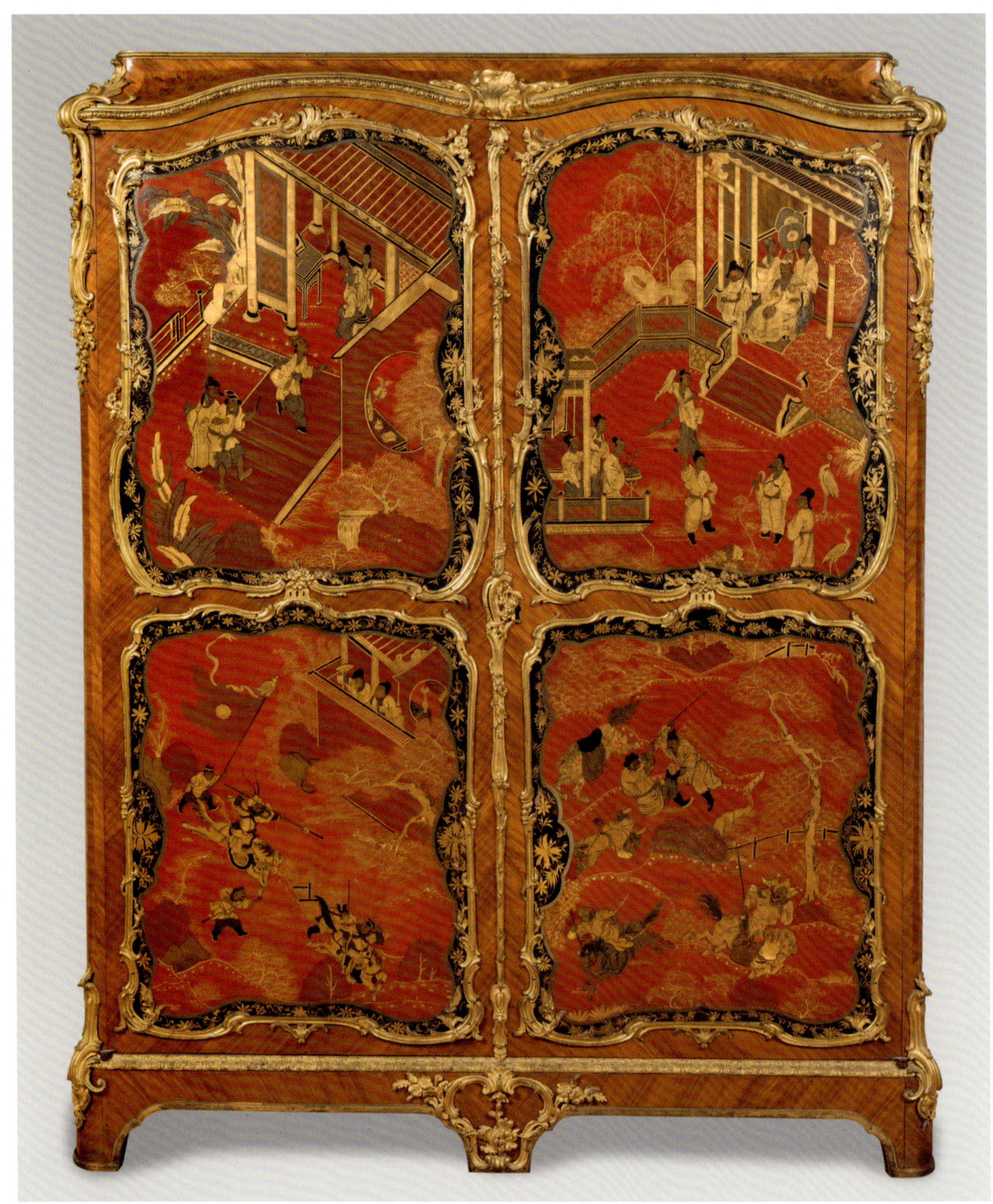

Fig. 27
Bernard van Risenburgh II
Armoire, ca. 1755
Oak, rosewood, purplewood, Chinese lacquer panels, European varnish, gilt-bronze mounts
h. 66 in. (167.4 cm), l. 54½ in. (138.5 cm), w. 15¾ in. (40.2 cm)
Musée du Louvre, Paris

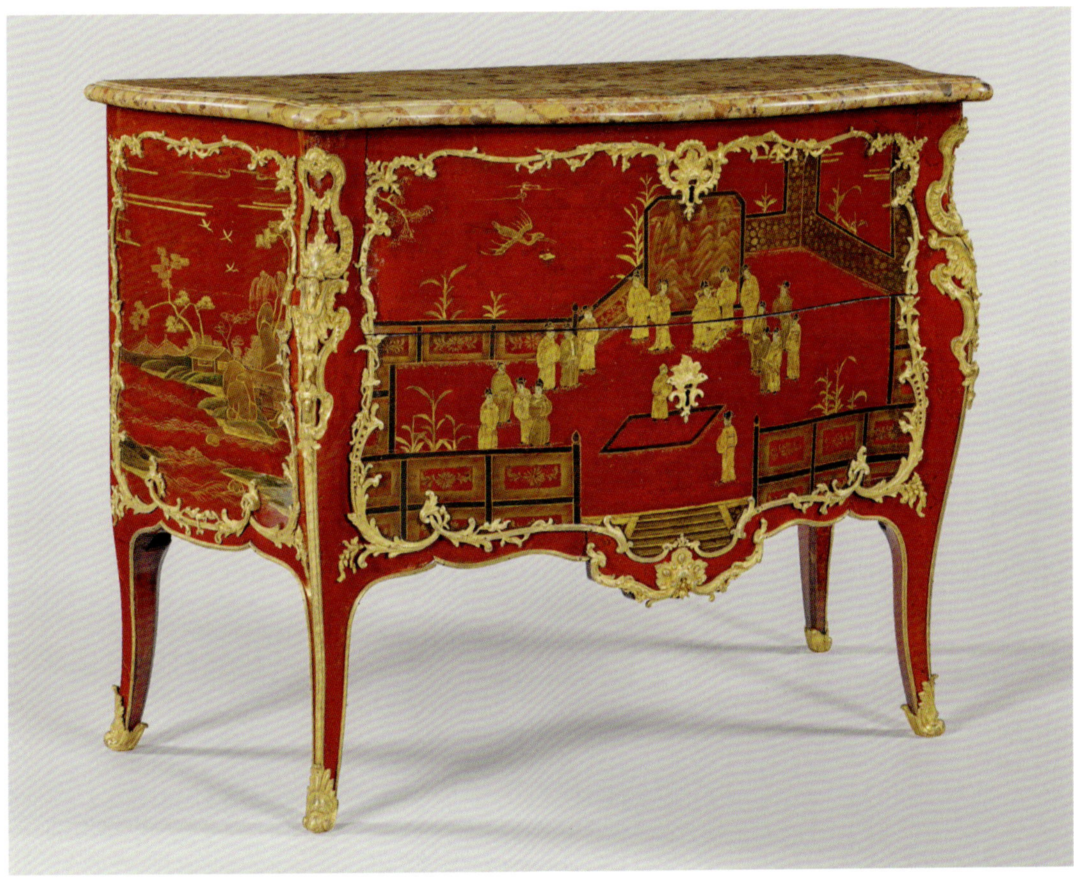

and stored in the Garde-Meuble de la Couronne.[51] This kind of reuse depended on the most skillful cabinetmakers, those capable of maintaining the integrity of the patterns and preventing the flat panels of fragile lacquer from cracking during the process. This was especially complicated by the curved lines and *bombé* (convex) surfaces characteristic of the style during the reign of Louis XV.[52] In his 1774 volume *Art du menuisier ébéniste* (Art of the Carpenter-Cabinetmaker), André Jacob Roubo (1739–1791) describes the entire process, including the precautions to take with veneer lacquer on furniture:

> Furniture is sometimes covered with lacquer or varnish from China or Japan, usually with a black ground and enhanced with gold ornaments. The lacquer we usually use in cabinetmaking is taken from Chinese or Japanese cabinets or screens from China or Japan that are, for the most part, varnished & painted on

Fig. 28
Bernard van Risenburgh II
Commode, ca. 1740
Oak set with panels of red Chinese lacquer on a coniferous substrate, sycamore maple painted with European lacquer, gilt-bronze mounts, brass and iron hardware and lock, Brèche d'Alep marble
h. 33 in. (83.8 cm), l. 45 in. (114.3 cm), w. 21⅝ in. (54.9 cm)
The J. Paul Getty Museum, Los Angeles

both sides, & which are split in half so they can then be reduced with a plane
& made ready to be veneered. . . . Great care must be taken both when cutting
these sheets, and when trimming them, for fear of splitting or splintering the
varnish; this is the reason why when being split, they must be placed in the
press between cushions or woolen blankets. . . . As far as possible, the joints of
lacquer works should be surrounded with brass mounts or borders because . . .
it is very difficult not to make a few splinters, which show the location of the
joints, which has a very bad effect; additionally, when you manage to cut the
lacquer as cleanly as possible, the edges of any openings that are not filled in
this way will soon get damaged, which always looks bad.[53]

The cabinetmakers often had to adjust the panels to make them fit, and
this could disrupt the harmony of the motif or scene depicted on the panel.
An example is the armoire (fig. 27) made by Bernard van Risenburgh II
around 1755 for Jean-Baptiste de Machault d'Arnouville, Controller-General
of Finances from 1745 and Keeper of the Seals and Minister of the Navy.[54]
The scenes, taken from what was initially a screen, are framed but are no
longer linked, unlike, for instance, in the commode with Chinese lacquer
panels he realized about ten years earlier (fig. 28).

A New Varnish

Sometimes, the panels provided to the cabinetmakers were not large enough
to cover the entire piece of furniture or to hide certain defects. That, together
with the demand for lacquerware and its high prices, led to the creation by
vernisseurs (varnishers) of materials that imitated lacquer.[55] Roubo briefly
mentions the use of such varnish:

In France, Chinese varnishes are imitated (as far as it has been possible until
the present time), which produces a more solid piece than those veneered
with Chinese lacquers. In the latter case, in other words, when we varnish
furniture, great care must be taken to ensure that the frames are made of
good wood, very dry, & extremely solid, as I have taught in the course of
this publication.[56]

Since at least 1670, most of the varnishers in Paris had been in the Faubourg
Saint-Antoine.[57] Several names can be traced: Paul Thévenard, Germain
Massot, Jean Ancellin, Nicolas Cibou, and Matthieu Langlois. Starting with
Guillaume Martin (1689–1749), who created and perfected the so-called

Vernis Martin, the Martins were one of the best-known families active in France.[58] In the July 1724 edition of the *Mercure de France*, it is recommended that those interested in work made in Chinese and Japanese varnish go to the *sieur* Martin, established on rue de Grenelle in Paris, as his craftsmanship surpassed anything at the time.[59] There seems to be no trace on the Frick commodes of vernis Martin or European varnish being used to make the transition between the delicately veneered panels, the gilt bronzes, and the rest of the surfaces. This could suggest that the use of tainted ebony, as well as the remarkable quality of the Japanese lacquer panels, was sufficient to achieve the same result. An example that illustrates the use of lacquer and Vernis Martin is a *Pair of Encoignures* (cupboards or corner cabinets) attributed to Bernard van Risenburgh II with the concave sides and lower cross both decorated with this type of varnish (fig. 29). Such varnish is sometimes even more visible, because unlike the Europeans, who put a high value on symmetry, the Japanese found

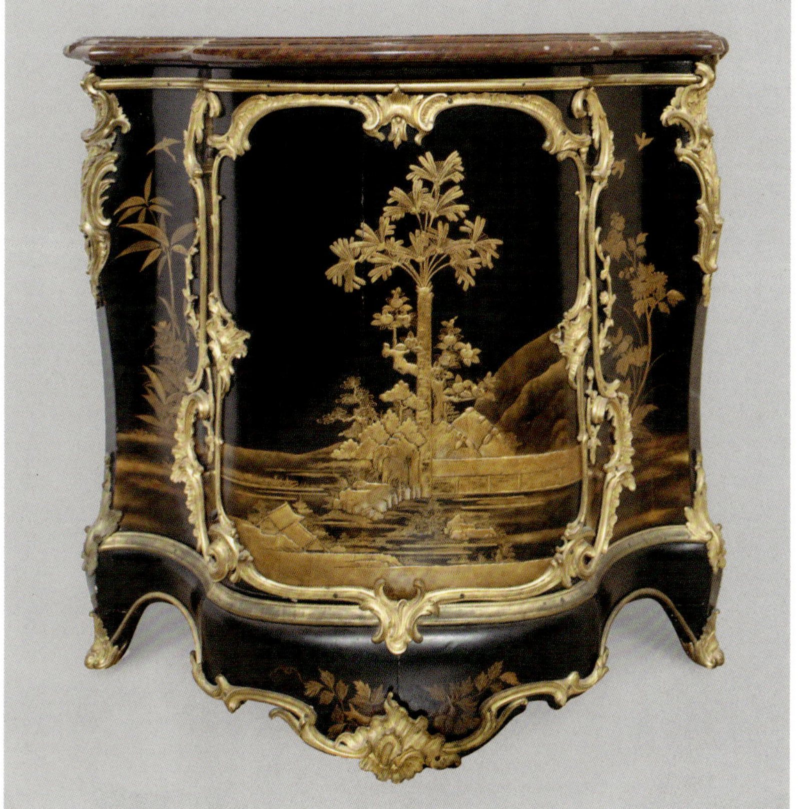

Fig. 29
Attributed to Bernard van Risenburgh II
Encoignure (one of a pair), ca. 1750
Oak veneered with Japanese lacquer and varnished; gilt-bronze mounts, red Griotte marble
h. 36¼ in. (92 cm), l. 28⅜ in. (72 cm), w. 36½ in. (93 cm)
Musée Nissim de Camondo, Paris

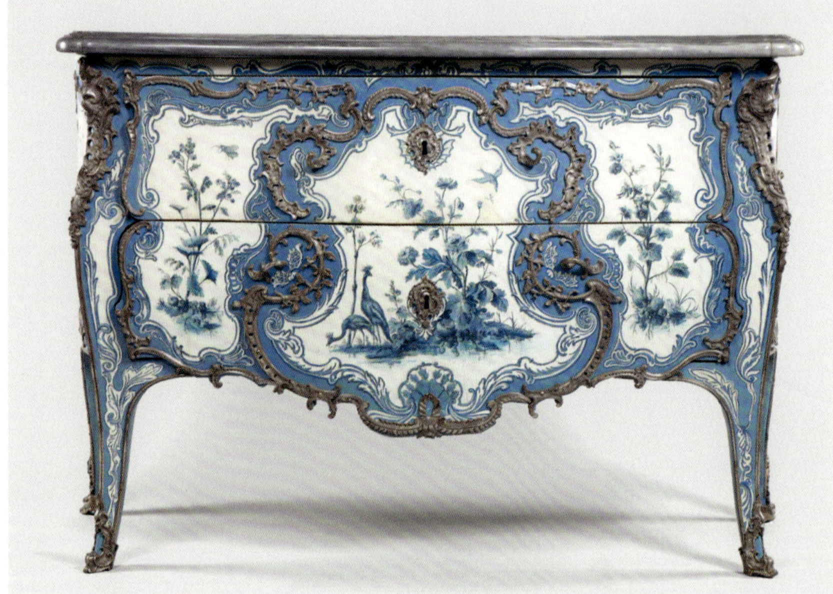

Fig. 30
Mathieu Criaerd
Commode, 1742
Oak, fruitwood, Vernis Martin,
gilt-bronze mounts, Bleu Turquin
marble
h. 33 ½ in. (85 cm), l. 52 in.
(132 cm), w. 25 ⅛ in. (63.8 cm)
Musée du Louvre, Paris

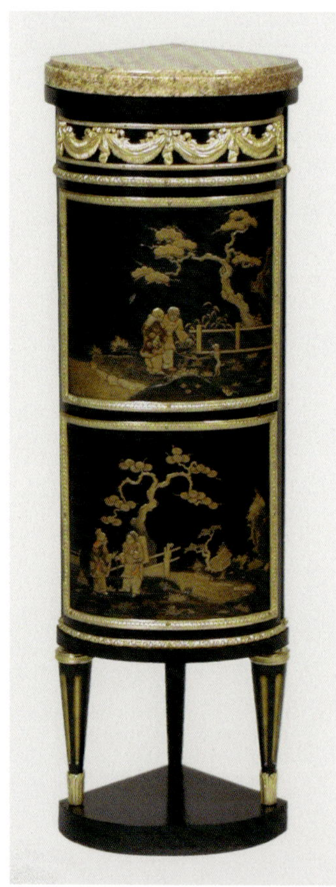
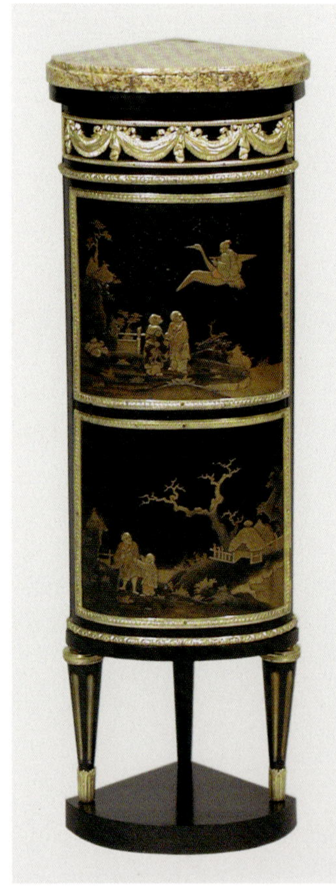

Fig. 31
Unknown artist
Pair of Small Encoignures, ca. 1775–80
Oak, ebony veneer, "black-and-gold" *tôle*,
gilt-bronze mounts, marble
h. 34 ⅜ in. (87.3 cm), w. 11 ⅜ in. (28.9 cm)
The Frick Collection, New York

beauty and harmony in large areas that remained empty.[60] Around 1750, the varnishers, including the Martin family, began to move away from the imitation of Chinese and Japanese lacquers to create new colored varnishes, as can be seen on a commode and *Pair of Encoignures* made in 1742 by Mathieu Criaerd (1689–1776) for the bedchamber of Madame de Mailly (1710–1751—Louis XV's favorite mistress—at the Château de Choisy, although the panels are very much inspired by Asia and and the work of painters like Boucher and Christophe Huet (fig. 30).[61] Later, *marchands merciers* also experimented with the use of Tôle Laquée, another imitative material—always with the goal of reducing costs and creating something new. This can be seen, for example, in a *Pair of Encoignures* formerly attributed to Martin Carlin (fig. 31) and on a commode with two doors made by Pierre Macret (1723–1806) around 1770 (fig. 32).[62]

Fig. 32
Pierre Macret
Commode, ca. 1770
Oak, varnished and lacquered sheet metal, amaranth and satin veneer
h. 34 13/16 in. (88.5 cm),
l. 53 ¾ in. (136.5 cm),
w. 24 ½ in. (62.2 cm)
Château de Versailles, Versailles

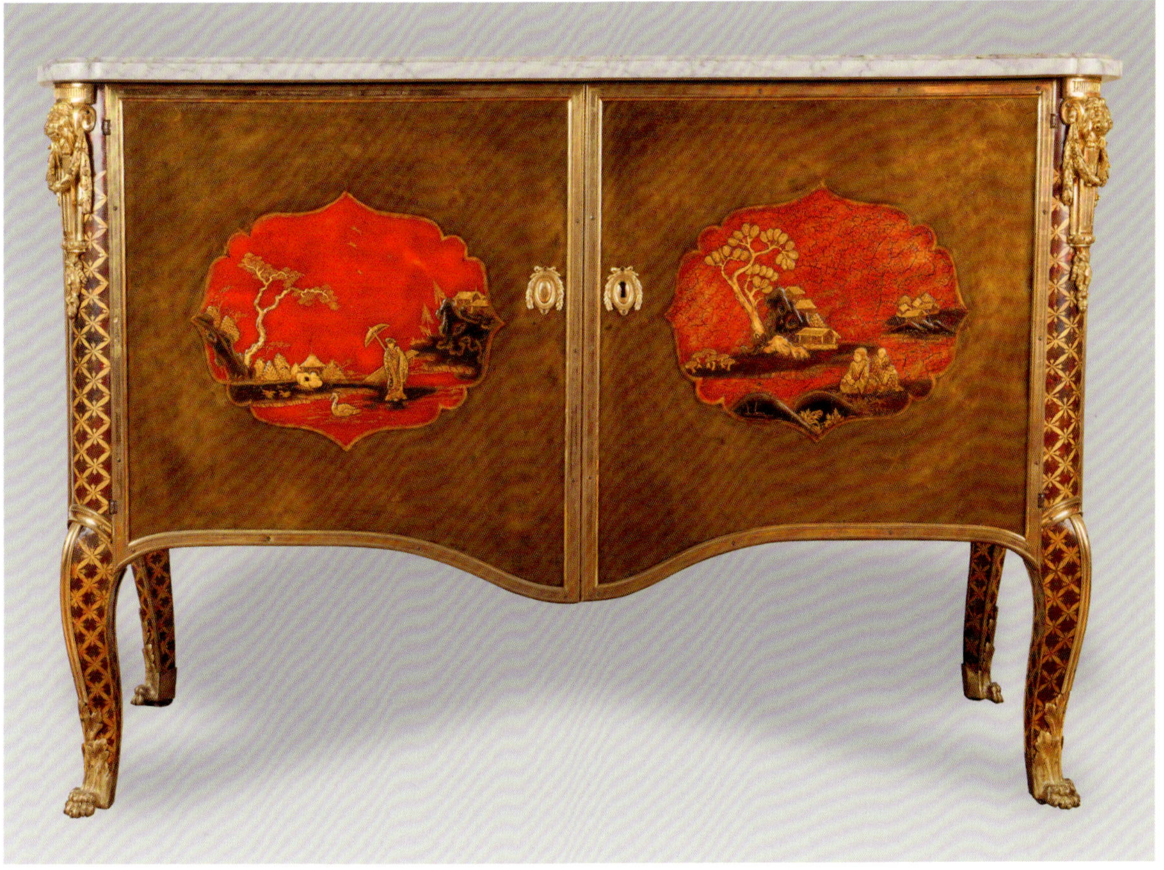

The Rise of Neoclassicism in Decorative Arts

The Frick's commodes were made during a pivotal time in the eighteenth century. Some theorists and important figures were beginning to disparage the excess of the popular *rocaille* (rococo) style favored in France in the 1750s in decorative arts and architectural ornaments (notably paneling). The engraver and critic Charles-Nicolas Cochin (1715–1790) vehemently criticized the impracticality of such a style in his "Supplication aux Orfèvres, Ciseleurs, Sculpteurs en bois pour les appartemens & autres, par une société d'Artistes" published in the December 1754 edition of the *Mercure de France*. He promoted a return to simplicity, proportions, and rigor:

> These gentlemen are therefore begged to observe from now on certain simple rules, which are dictated by common sense. . . . It would be a very meritorious act . . . if they would be willing to lend themselves to our weakness and forgive us for the real possibility we are in to destroy, out of indulgence for them, all the lights of our reason. For example, silversmiths are asked, when they execute on the lid of a *pot à oille* (tureen) or on any other piece of silver an artichoke or a stalk of celery of natural size, not to place next to it a hare as large as a finger, a real-size lark, and a pheasant a quarter or a fifth its size; children the same size as a vine leaf; figures supposed to be of natural size, carried on an ornamental leaf, which can barely support a small bird; trees whose trunk is as tiny as one of their leaves, & a quantity of other things equally logical. We would still be infinitely obliged to them if they would not change the destination of things, & remember, for example, that a candlestick must be straight and perpendicular to carry the light, & not be twisted, as if someone had forced it; that a *bobèche* must be concave to receive the wax that flows, & not convex to make it fall on the candlestick, & a host of other no less unreasonable examples it would be too long to recite.[63]

Cochin may have had a point, and one could wonder how practical the superb series of models for silver candlesticks—including several intended for the king—by Juste-Aurèle Meissonnier (1695–1750) could have been (fig. 33).[64] The *bobèche*—the part of a candlestick made to catch wax—would hardly contain the wax slowly dripping from the flame. Although the design is meant to be adapted when the silversmith makes the object, the style of Meissonnier and his contemporaries—Claude II Ballin (1661–1754), Jacques Roëttiers (1707–1784), and François-Thomas Germain (1726–1791), who were all appointed *orfèvres du Roi* (goldsmiths to the king)—was still strongly

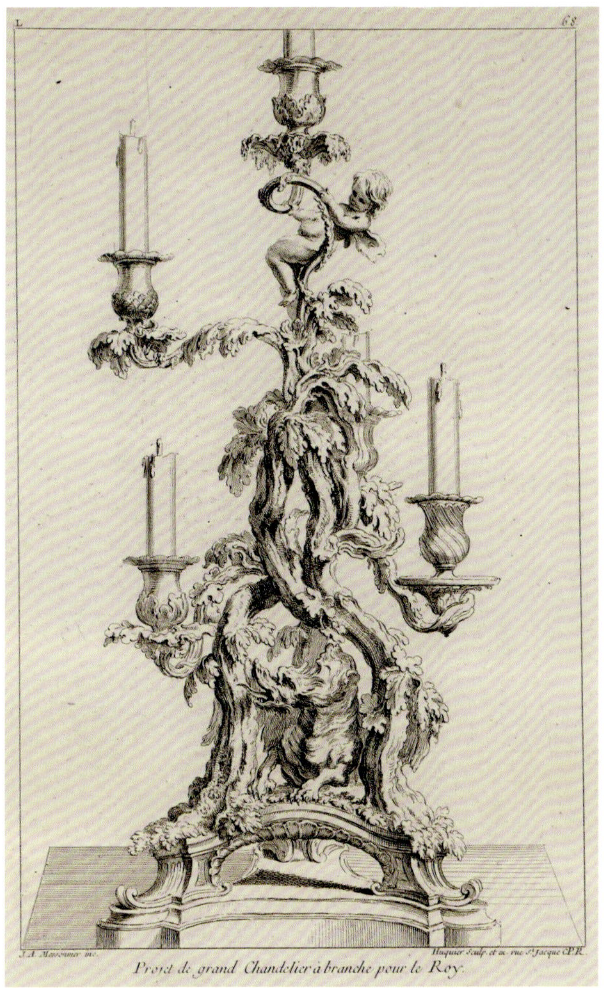

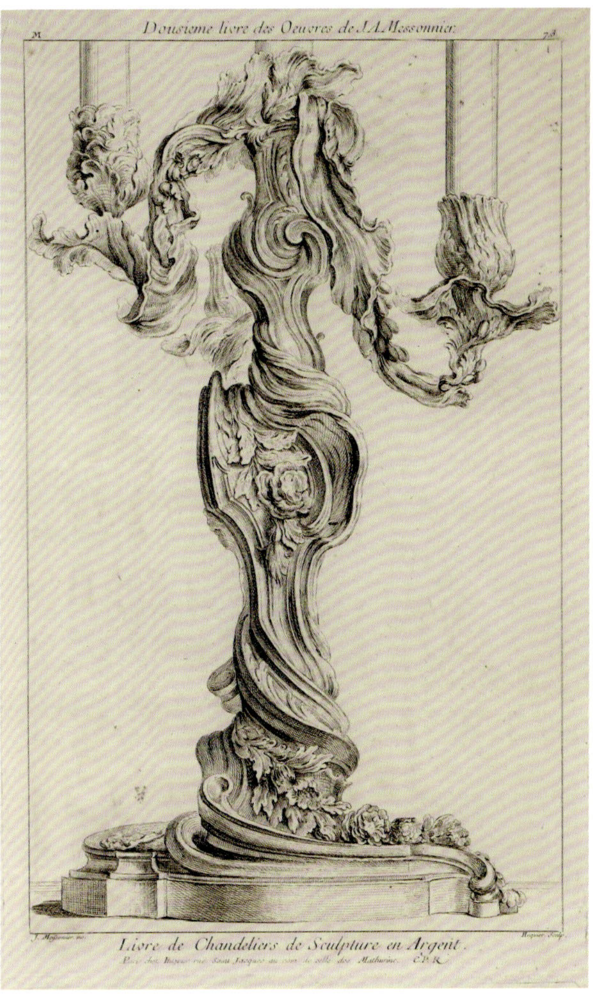

characterized by the curves and counter-curves inherent in the *rocaille* style (fig. 34).[65] These debates led to a period of transition before the emergence of a new style called *goût grec* (Greek taste), inspired by the excavations in Italy and the rediscovery of Herculaneum in 1709 and Pompeii in 1738, which aroused immense interest in aristocratic circles in Europe. The *goût grec* flourished in France, thanks to Abel-François Poisson de Vandières (1727–1781)—marquis de Marigny (from 1754) and the brother of Madame de Pompadour—who became Director General of the King's Buildings in 1751. The marquis de Marigny possessed a keen interest in this new style after his sister had organized a two-year trip to Italy to see the antiquities with

Fig. 33
Juste-Aurèle Meissonnier
Design for a candelstick for
King Louis XV, in *Œuvre de
Juste Aurele Meissonnier peintre
sculpteur architecte & dessinateur
de la chambre et du cabinet du roy
(première partie executée sous la
conduitte de l'auteur)*, ca. 1745 (?)
Etching, h. 23 in. (58.5 cm)
Bibliothèque de l'Institut
National de l'Histoire de l'Art,
Paris

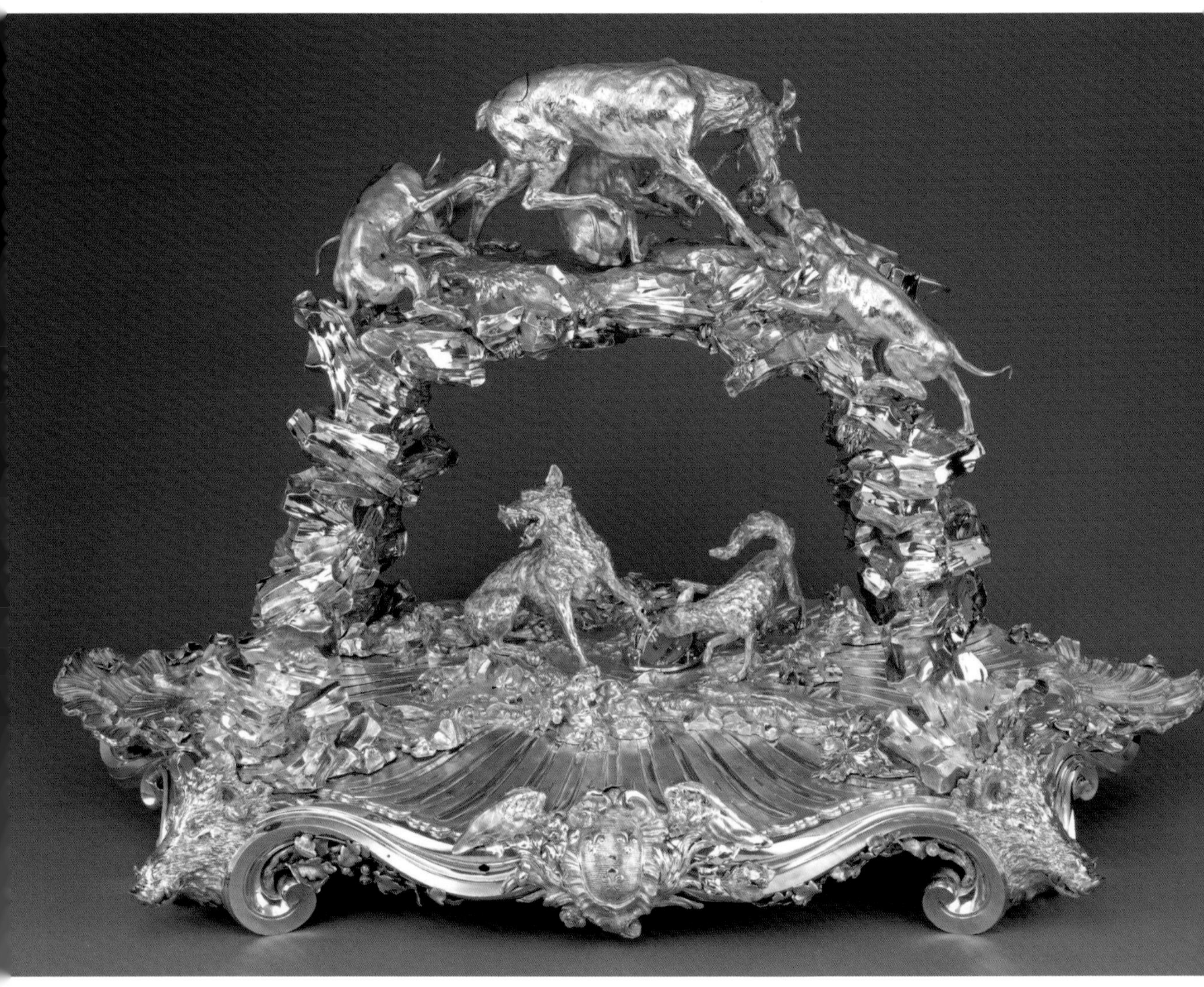

Fig. 34
Jacques Roëttiers
Surtout de table, ca. 1734–35
Silver
h. 24 ½ in. (62 cm), l. 37 in. (94 cm), w. 24 ½ in. (62 cm)
Musée du Louvre, Paris

Cochin and the architect Jacques-Germain Soufflot (1713–1780).[66] In fact, in 1766, Poirier delivered to Marigny a Baumhauer commode *à la grecque* (in the Greek taste), veneered with Japanese lacquer and featuring gilt bronzes, including a Vitruvian *frise* (fig. 35).[67]

The gilt bronzes illustrating musical instruments on the Frick commodes mirror some debates occurring at the time in the music world. A quarrel was sparked by the performance of the comic opera *La serva padrona* (The Servant Mistress), by Giovanni Battista Pergolesi (1710–1736), which premiered in 1733 and was presented again in 1752 at the Académie Royale de Musique. Later termed the "Querelle des Bouffons" or "Guerre des Bouffons" (the Quarrel or War of the Comic Actors), the dispute saw musicians, composers, and men of letters arguing to defend their philosophy of music in France. On the one side, Friedrich Melchior, Baron von Grimm (1723–1807), and others praised the French style of Rameau and vehemently criticized the Italian influence on French music that had started with Jean-Baptiste Lully (1632–1687) under the reign of Louis XIV. On the other side was Jean-Jacques Rousseau (1712–1778), among others, who defended Pergolesi's style. In any

Fig. 35
Joseph Baumhauer (known as Joseph)
Commode à la grecque, ca. 1766
Approximate h. 34 ¼ in. (87 cm), l. 63 in. (160 cm), w. 24 ½ in. (62 cm)
Private collection

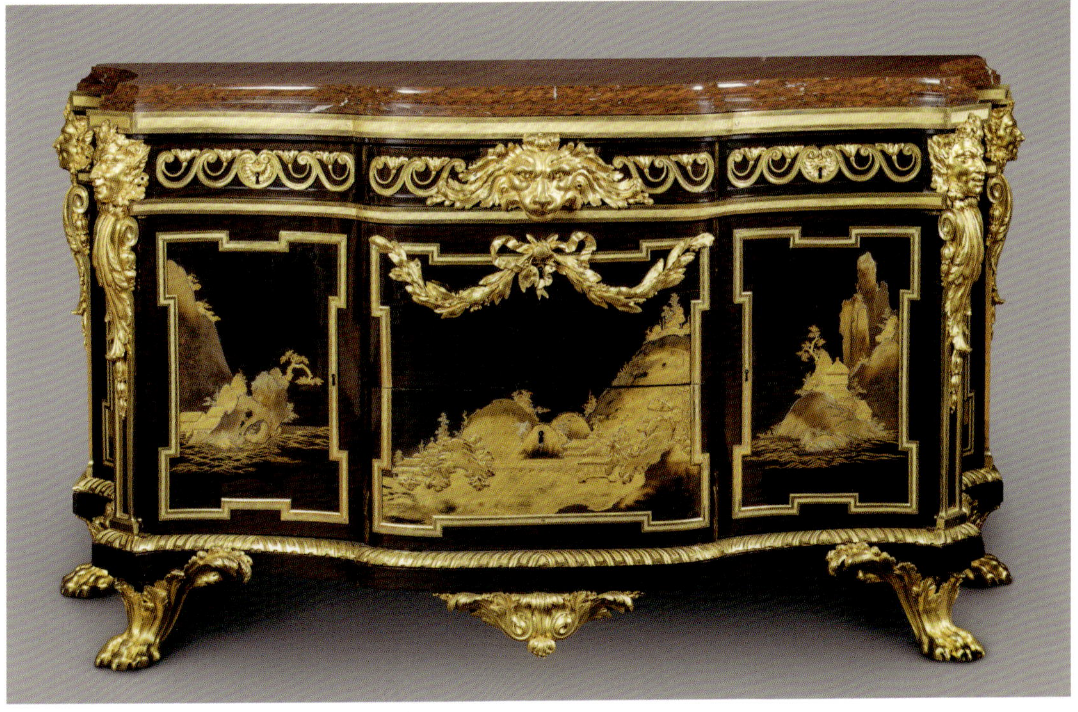

Fig. 36
Joseph Baumhauer (known as Joseph)
Bureau-cartonnier (Desk with Filing Cabinet), ca. 1757–60
Oak, ebony, gilt-bronze mounts, leather
desk, h. 34 ¼ in. (87 cm), l. 76 ⅝ in. (194.7 cm), w. 42 ⁵⁄₁₆ in. (107.5 cm)
cartonnier, h. 61 ⅞ in. (157 cm), l. 11 ⅞ in. (30 cm), w. 10 ¹⁄₁₆ in. (25.5 cm)
clock, h. 23 ½ in. (60 cm), l. 11 ¹³⁄₁₆ in. (30 cm), w. 10 ¹⁄₁₆ in. (25.5 cm)
Château de Chantilly, Chantilly

event, in earlier works, Rameau started to include various elements of the Italian style in his compositions, such as the opera *Platée* (1745), and the quarrel was resolved within months, as French music slowly began to absorb elements coming from Italy.[68]

In the world of decorative arts, one of the first pieces of furniture to fully express the *goût grec* is a *bureau* (desk) with a *cartonnier* (filing cabinet) made by Baumhauer, now at Chantilly. Intended for the influential collector Ange-Laurent de Lalive de Jully (1725–1779) (fig. 36), the piece is richly adorned with gilt bronzes after drawings by Louis-Joseph Le Lorrain (1715–1759) inspired by antiquity by Philippe Caffiéri (1714–1774).[69] Other talented cabinetmakers embraced the style: a commode *à la grecque* made by Jean-François Oeben around 1760 for Madame de Pompadour, commissioned for her small chateau in Menars (fig. 37), offers a stark contrast to the mechanical table by Oeben, completed by his brother-in-law, Roger Vandercruse Lacroix,

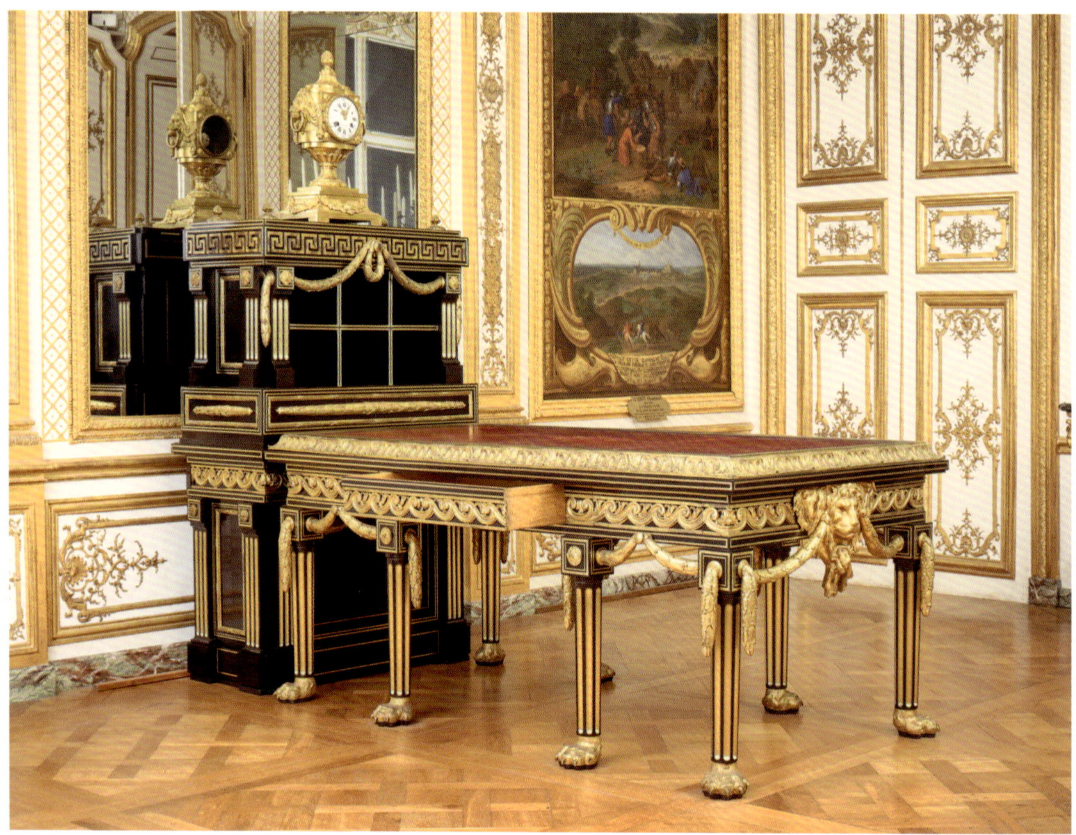

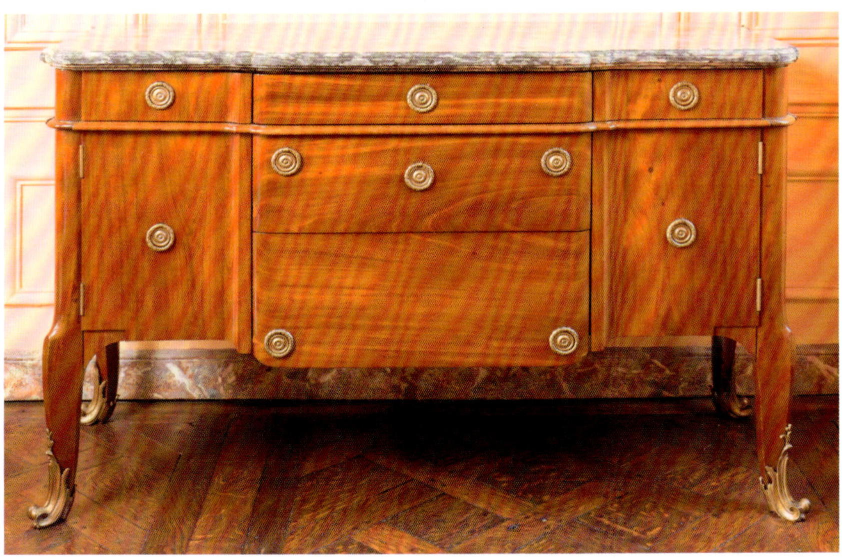

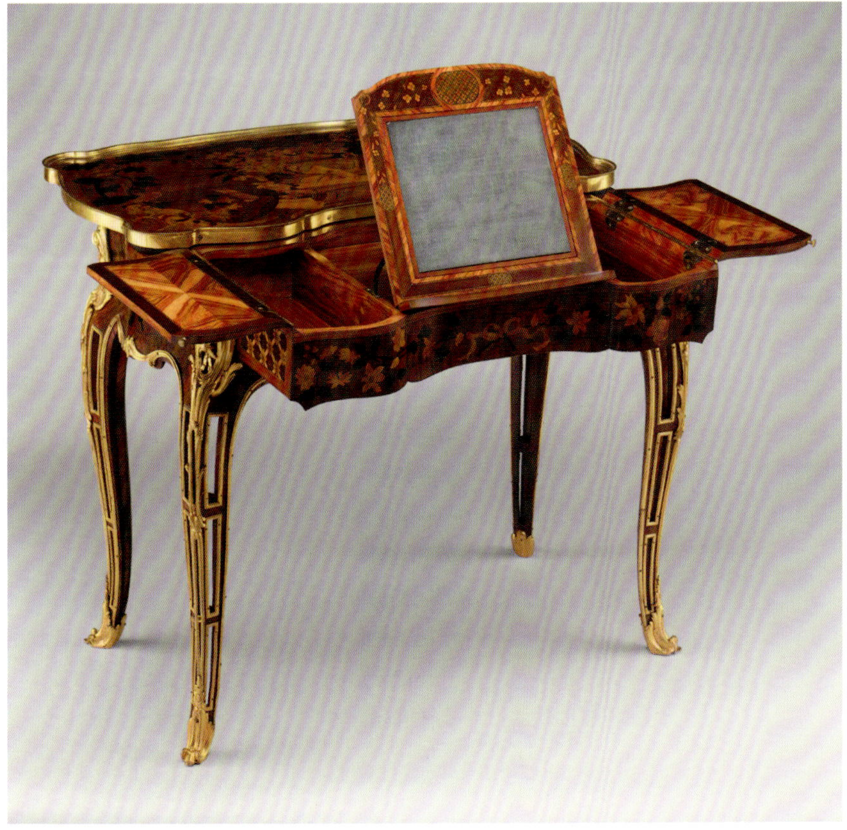

Fig. 37
Jean-François Oeben
Commode à la grecque,
ca. 1760–63
Oak, mahogany, red Mayenne
marble, gilt-bronze mounts
h. 33 1/16 in. (84 cm), l. 52 in.
(132 cm), w. 22 1/16 in. (56 cm)
Private collection

Fig. 38
Jean-François Oeben and Roger
Vandercruse Lacroix known as
RVLC
Mechanical Table, ca. 1761–63
Oak veneered with mahogany,
kingwood, tulipwood, marquetry
of mahogany, rosewood, holly,
and various other woods,
gilt-bronze mounts, imitation
Japanese lacquer, replaced silk
h. 27 1/2 in. (69.9 cm), l. 32 1/4 in.
(81.9 cm), w. 18 3/8 in. (46.7 cm)
The Metropolitan Museum of
Art, New York

and delivered around the same time (fig. 38). The Oeben table still embraces the playfulness of the *rocaille* style with the asymmetrical motifs on the marquetery depicting trophies of architecture, music, and love, and additionally combining these elements with the complex and elaborate treatment of the legs, whereas the commode reflects a transition toward neoclassicism, which prized classical antiquity and valued simplicity, symmetry, and even rigor.[70]

* * *

The pair of Frick commodes attributed to BVRB II and his son BVRB III reflects the talents of a generation of cabinetmakers who worked almost exclusively for Parisian *marchands merciers* and whose prestigious clientele ranged from the royal family and the court to *financiers* in Paris mostly residing in the Faubourg Saint-Honoré. The cabinets are a testament to the ingenuity of men such as Lazare Duvaux, Thomas-Joachim Hébert, and Simon-Philippe Poirier who belonged to a guild that ceaselessly found ways to introduce new goods to the luxury market during the eighteenth century. Finally, the commodes illustrate the taste for Asian lacquerware and more generally for the so-called chinoiseries in France but also in Europe. This trend remained across multiple fields. In decorative arts, the Sèvres manufactory created porcelain pieces with a *fond noir et chinoiseries* (black ground and chinoiseries), which imitated Asian lacquerware and pieces made to resemble Tôle Vernie and Vernis Martin. Several tapestry subjects alluded to Asia, for instance, the "Seconde tenture chinoise" woven at the Beauvais manufactory from 1743 to 1775 after cartoons by François Boucher, who was himself an avid collector of Chinese and Japanese objects. In architecture, eighteenth-century collectors Henri Léonard Bertin and Étienne François de Choiseul built a Chinese pavilion and a pagoda, respectively, on their estates. The taste persisted throughout the nineteenth and twentieth centuries in these fields, in architecture with the presence of Chinese rooms and pavilions and in classical music with the oeuvre of Claude Debussy, who was greatly influenced by Japan in works such as *La Mer* (The Sea) composed in 1905 and by Indonesia in *Pagodes*, a musical work part of his *Estampes* (Prints) and completed two years earlier.[71] Henry Clay Frick's acquisition of these commodes, as well as the few pieces of Chinese porcelain he acquired before his death, demonstrate the continued interest in and history of collecting of Chinese and Japanese works from the seventeenth and eighteenth centuries.

Notes

1 Originally cast in bronze, the sculpture was made after a
design by the sculptor Eugène Guillaume. It was melted
down in 1942–43 by the Vichy regime that collaborated
with the Nazi occupiers. A stone reproduction was made
in 1950 and installed on the place de la Sainte-Chapelle
before being moved to the place de la Libération in June
2016. The statue is currently located on the boulevard
Georges Clemenceau.

2 The *tragédie en musique* (musical tragedy) is a genre made
popular in France by Jean-Baptiste Lully (1632–1687).

3 Baroli 1957.

4 See "Spectacles" 1735a, 1851; "Spectacles" 1735b,
2035–47. The following year, a fourth act was added. See
"Spectacles" 1736a, 343; "Spectacles" 1736b, 534–39.

5 The opera-ballet consists of a prologue and four *entrées*,
or acts: Act 1, *Le Turc généreux* (The Generous Turk); Act
2, *Les Incas du Pérou* (The Incas of Peru); Act 3, *Les Fleurs
ou la Fête persane* (The Flowers or Persian Celebration);
and Act 4, *Les Sauvages* (The Savages). The opera, with the
addition of Act 4, premiered at the Académie Royale de
Musique in Paris on March 10, 1736. For the production
at the Comédie-Italienne, see "Spectacles" 1725.

6 See *Mercure de France* 1765, 36–40.

7 This embassy was initially larger, but ultimately only four
made the journey to France after the ship chartered by
the Compagnie Française pour le Commerce des Indes
Orientales (French East India Company) sank near the
shores of Dauphine Island, according to the *Mercure de
France*. The trip had two objectives. France was seeking to
consolidate or expand the territory conquered in North
America, and the Native American nations were seeking
French protection (they also had access to European
weapons) in their conflicts with other nations. For this
visit and the festivities during their stay in France, see
"Relation" 1725.

8 Ibid., esp. 2830–31.

9 Ibid. On the presence of foreigners at the court and the
impression they made, see Sanson 2016.

10 See Fuzelier 1735.

11 On the fascination with Asia and its trade of porcelain
and lacquerware, see Castelluccio 2019a; Castelluccio
2013; Paris 2014, 11–18. See also Versailles 2014b,
60–85, 120–39, and 190–247. On the use of
Coromandel lacquer in Europe, see Brugier 2015,
177–207.

12 "Deux riches Bas d'armoire, ouvrant chacun à deux
ventaux garnis de Panneaux de laque du Japon, à dessins

de figures de Chinois, Plantes et Arbustes en relief et en
or sur fond noir. Ils sont garnis de divers ornemens de
bon genre, comme console renversée, guirlande de chêne,
trophées de musique et pied; le tout en bronze de bonne
ciselure et doré d'or moulu. Leur dessus est de marbre
tarentais, dont un est agraffé"; *Catalogue de tableaux* 1803,
166, no. 342.

13 Dell 1992, 295–313.

14 Ibid., 295.

15 Ibid., 295–96.

16 Due to the family's foreign origins, we find multiple
spellings for their family name: van Riesen Burgh, van
Risen Burgh, vanrisamburgh, van Risamburgh.

17 Alexandre Pradère (1989a, 183) also notes that BVRB I
brought a dowry of 4,000 *livres* for the marriage of his
daughter Marie-Anne-Marguerite in 1722.

18 Castelluccio 2019a, 8.

19 Baroli 1957, 59.

20 For Charles Cressent's production, see Pradère 2003.

21 Wolvesperges 2000, 245.

22 For BVRB II and the dynasty, see Chuang 2020. I would
like to thank Grace Chuang for taking the time to discuss
her research with me.

23 I am grateful to Jenny Saunt, Senior Curator in charge
of furniture and woodwork at the Victoria and Albert
Museum, for showing me the commode in the galleries.

24 On the commode with Coromandel lacquer attributed to
BVRB II, see Versailles 2014a, 134–35.

25 Courajod 1873.

26 Versailles 2014a, 166–69.

27 Pradère 1989a, 185; Vente de fond 1764. For the
furniture ready to be veneered with lacquer in
BVRB II's workshop, see Wolvesperges 2000, 148.
Wolvesperges compares BVRB II's financial situation to
that of the cabinetmaker Jacques Dubois, whose widow
continued his workshop after his death before selling it
in July 1772 to his son, René Dubois, for 25,000 *livres*;
Wolvesperges 2000, 308.

28 Ibid.

29 Baroli 1957, 61.

30 See Dell 1992, 295–313. See also Vignon 2015, 90.

31 See Dell 1992, 302; and Wolvesperges 2000, 245. See
also AN, 389: "Deux batis de Commodes Entique sur lun
desquels sont commancés a monter les Cadres des portes
et coté et les moulures du haut et du bas en Cuivre."

32 Pradère 1989a, 198–99.

33 Wolvesperges 2000, 203–4.

34 See Castelluccio 2013, 2019a, and 2019b. On gifts sent to China in the eighteenth century, see Rochebrune 2019, Finlay 2019, and Smentek 2019. On gifts exchanged between China and France, see Zhao and Simon 2019. For turqueries in France and Europe, see Bély 2009 and Williams 2014.

35 The reception of the second Ottoman embassy in France in 1742 is best viewed in the context of the War of the Austrian Succession (1740–48), as France hoped to receive military support from the Ottomans against the Habsburgs. For the diplomatic relations between the Ottoman Empire and France, see Poumarède 2009 and 2020. See also Veinstein 2014, *Mercure de France* 1742, and "Suite de l'Ambassade" 1743. On the gifts exchanged during the second Ottoman embassy sent to France in 1742, see AAE, fols. 140–43.

36 Other species of trees in Southeast Asia from which lacquer is made include *Rhus succedanea* in Vietnam and *Melanorrhoea usitata* and *M. laccifera* in Cambodia, Laos, Thailand, and Myanmar.

37 Wolvesperges 2000, 135–45. The Dutch alone had access to the market in Japan after the Portuguese were expelled in 1640.

38 The use of lacquer can be traced back to the Shang dynasty in China (ca. 1600–1045 BCE); Castelluccio 2019a, 17. See also Brugier 2015, 5–12; S. Castelluccio in Paris 2014, 19–31.

39 Castelluccio 2019a, 20–21.

40 See Versailles 2017, 158–60.

41 Castelluccio 2019a, 38, 171–72. See also Sargentson 1996, 62–63.

42 Castelluccio 2019a, 169–72.

43 Ibid., 63–66. On the Garde-Meuble de la Couronne and its organization, see Castelluccio 2022.

44 These lacquer pieces were sold in Coromandel, on the southeastern coast of India, but the main centers of production remained in China. Brugier 2015, 18–21. See also Wolvesperges 2000, 52–57.

45 Brugier 2015, 92–93. See also Wolvesperges 2000, 145.

46 Le Rond d'Alembert and Diderot 1765, 369. For luxury goods and the role of the *marchands merciers* in eighteenth-century France, see Verlet 1958, Sargentson 1996, and Paris 2018, as well as Castelluccio 2014, Coquery 2004, and Coquery 2006. See also the publications of Daniel Roche (1989 and 1997), who analyzed eighteenth-century material culture among the French aristocracy and elites.

47 See also Glorieux 2002.

48 "Gersaint Marchand Jouaillier sur le Pont Nôtre Dame vend toute sorte de Clainquaillerie [*sic*] Nouvelle et de Gout, Bijoux, Glaces, Tableaux de Cabinet, Pagodes, Vernis et Porcelaines du Japon, Coquillages et autres morceaux d'Histoire Naturelle, Cailloux, Agathes, et generalement toutes Marchandises Curieuses et Etrangeres."

49 On *financiers*, *fermiers généraux*, and their rise to power during the reigns of Louis XIV and Louis XV, see Dessert 1984 and 2012 and Durand 1971.

50 On the collaboration between Gaudreaus and the *marchand mercier* Hébert, see Vittet 2009.

51 Alcouffe 1985. See, more recently, Alcouffe, Grall, and Perfettini 2022.

52 Regarding the composition of lacquer on eighteenth century furniture, see Chasen et al. 2021, 9–16.

53 "On revêtit quelquefois les meubles avec de la laque ou vernis de la Chine ou du Japon, dont ordinairement le fond est noir & rehaussé d'ornements d'or. La laque qu'on emploie ordinairement en Ebénisterie, se prend dans des feuilles soit de cabinet ou de paravent venu de la Chine ou du Japon, qui, pour la plupart, sont vernies & peintes des deux côtés, & qu'on refend au milieu de leur épaisseur pour les diminuer ensuite au rabot & les mettre en état d'être plaquées sur des fonds de Menuiserie ordinaire. Il faut prendre beaucoup de précautions tant pour refendre ces feuilles, que pour les diminuer, de crainte de faire fendre ou éclatter le vernis; c'est pourquoi, lorqu'on les refend, il faut les mettre dans la presse entre des coussins ou des couvertures de laine. Il faut avoir la même précaution lorsqu'on les rabote par derrière, c'est-à-dire, qu'il faut sur l'établi une couverture ployée en double, pour que les inégalités qui sont à la surface du vernis à l'endroit des fleurs ou autres ornements, entrent dans l'épaisseur de cette couverture. En diminuant l'épaisseur des bois qui portent la laque ou vernis de la Chine, il faut prendre garde de leur laisser assez de consistance pour qu'ils ne se rompent pas; c'est pourquoi il faut leur laisser au moins une ligne d'épaisseur; après quoi on les plaque sur l'ouvrage à l'ordinaire, en prenant toutefois la précaution de les faire chauffer, ainsi que les bâtis qui doivent les recevoir, & d'étendre sur la laque des couvertures, par-dessus lesquelles on met des coussins ou des calles de bois avec des goberges ou des presses à coller, selon qu'on le juge nécessaire; mais il ne faut jamais se servir de valets pour faire ces collages, de crainte qu'en frappant dessus pour les serrer, on n'étonne le vernis, & qu'on ne le fasse fendre. Autant qu'il est possible, on

entoure les joints des ouvrages de laque de rapport avec des ornemens ou des cadres de cuivres, parce que quelques précautions qu'on prenne en coupant les feuilles de laque, il est bien difficile de n'y pas faire quelques éclats, qui font paroître la place des joints, ce qui fait un très-mauvais effet; de plus, quand on pourroit parvenir à couper la laque avec toute la propreté possible, les arêtes des ouvertures qui se seroient pas ainsi garnies, ne tarderoient pas à être gâtées, ce qui feroit toujours mal"; Roubo 1774, 1020–21. See also Wolvesperges 2000, 59–67.

54 Versailles 2014a, 156–57. On his estate and possessions, see also Pruchnicki 2013.

55 During the seventeenth century, the *vernisseur* Étienne Sager (d. 1633) was appointed *maître faiseur d'ouvrages de la Chine* (master making work in the Chinese manner) by Marie de' Medici (1575–1642). Sager specialized in making small objects. See Paris 2014, 14–16; Wolvesperges 2000, 89.

56 "On imite en France les vernis de la Chine (du moins autant bien qu'il a été possible jusqu'à présent) ce qui fait de l'ouvrage plus solide que celui où on plaque ceux de la Chine. Dans ce dernier cas, c'est-à-dire, quand on vernit les meubles, il faut avoir grand soin que leurs bâtis soient construits de bon bois très-sec, & avec toute la solidité possible, comme je l'ai enseigné dans le cours de cet Ouvrage"; Roubo 1774, 1021.

57 D. Alcouffe in Paris 2014, 33–43.

58 Paris 2014, 45–122. See also Wolvesperges 2000, 17–29, 89–129.

59 *Mercure de France* 1724, 1583.

60 Castelluccio 2019a, 157–61.

61 See Versailles 2014a, 138–41; Bimbenet-Privat, Dassas, and Durand 2015, 256–57.

62 The *Pair of Small Encoignures* at the Frick are under the accession number 1914.5.144–45. For the career of Pierre Macret and his production, see Giraud 2022.

63 "Soit très-humblement représenté à ces Messieurs, que quelques efforts que la Nation Françoise ait fait depuis plusieurs années pour accoutumer sa raison à se plier aux écarts de leur imagination, elle n'a pû y parvenir entierement: ces Messieurs sont donc supliés de vouloir bien dorénavant observer certaines règles simples, qui sont dictées par le bon sens, & dont nous ne pouvons arracher les principes de notre esprit. Ce seroit un acte bien méritoire à ces Messieurs, que de vouloir bien se prêter à notre foiblesse, & nous pardonner l'impossibilité réelle où nous sommes de détruire, par complaisance pour eux, toutes les lumieres de notre raison. Exemple. Sont priés les Orfèvres, lorsque sur le couvercle d'un pot à ouille ou sur quelqu'autre pièce d'orfevrerie, ils exécutent un artichaut ou un pied de céleri de grandeur naturelle, de vouloir bien ne pas mettre à côté un lievre grand comme le doigt, une allouette grande comme le naturel, & un faisan du quart ou du cinquième de sa grandeur; des enfants de la même grandeur qu'une feuille de vigne; des figures supposées de grandeur naturelle, portées sur une feuille d'ornement, qui pourroit à peine soutenir sans plier un petit oiseau; des arbres dont le tronc n'est pas si gros qu'une de leurs feuilles, & quantité d'autres choses également bien raisonnées. Nous leur serions encore infiniment obligés s'ils vouloient bien ne pas changer la destination des choses, & se souvenir, par exemple, qu'un chandelier doit être droit et perpendiculaire pour porter la lumiere, & non pas tortué, comme si quelqu'un l'avoit forcé; qu'une bobeche doit être concave pour recevoir la cire qui coule, & non pas convexe pour la faire tomber en nape sur le chandelier, & quantité d'autres agrémens non moins déraisonnables qu'il seroit trop long de citer." See "Supplication" 1754, 178–80, for this specific passage in French.

64 For Meissonnier's production, see Fuhring 1999.

65 For the career and production of François-Thomas Germain, see Perrin 1993. See also Bapst 1887.

66 See Eriksen 1962. See also Blois 2012.

67 Wolvesperges 2000, 202–3.

68 *Platée* was presented at Versailles during the festivities celebrating the marriage of the dauphin and heir apparent, Louis of France (1729–1765), to the infanta Maria Teresa of Spain (1726–1746). In *Platée*, Rameau was starting to include various elements of the Italian style, for instance by making the figure of Platée and the gods objects of derision, as might be seen in an Italian *opera buffa*.

69 Wolvesperges 2000, 199–238.

70 See Pradère 1989a, 260, and Pradère 1989b. See also Versailles 2014a, 188.

71 Debussy's music remained also in the lineage of Rameau, as acknowledged by Alfred Cortot in *La Musique française de piano* (1930).

BIBLIOGRAPHY

AAE Archives du Ministère des Affaires Étrangères, série Mémoire et Documents (France), vol. 2097.

AN Archives Nationales, Minutier Central, XXVIII.

Alcouffe 1985 Alcouffe, Daniel. "Antoine-Robert Gaudreaus et François Antoine-Robert Gaudreaus, ébénistes de Louis XV." *Antologia di belle arti, Mélanges Verlet: Studi sulle arti decorative in Europa*, no. 27–28 (1985): 73–97.

Alcouffe, Grall, and Perfettini 2022 Alcouffe, Daniel, Elisabeth Grall, and Jean Perfettini, eds. *Antoine Robert Gaudreaus: Ébéniste de Louis XV*. Dijon, 2022.

Bapst 1887 Bapst, Germain. *Étude sur l'orfèvrerie française au XVIII⁰ siècle. Les Germain, orfèvres-sculpteurs du roi*. Paris, 1887.

Baroli 1957 Baroli, Jean-Pierre. "Le mystérieux B.V.R.B enfin identifié." *Connaissance des Arts*, no. 61 (1957): 56–63.

Bély 2009 Bély, Lucien, ed. *Turcs et turqueries (XVI⁰–XVIII⁰ siècles)*. Paris, 2009.

Bimbenet-Privat, Dassas, and Durand 2015 Bimbenet-Privat, Michèle, Frédéric Dassas, and Jannic Durand, eds. *Decorative Furnishings and Objets d'Art in the Louvre from Louis XIV to Marie-Antoinette*. Paris, 2015.

Blois 2012 Rabreau, Daniel. "Marigny, maître d'ouvrage au nom du roi, réformateur du gout." In *Le naturel exalté: Marigny, Ministre des arts au château de Menars*, edited by Christophe Morin, 40–63. Exh. cat. Blois (Expo 41), 2012.

Brugier 2015 Brugier, Nicole. *Les Laques de Coromandel*. Lausanne, 2015.

Castelluccio 2004 Castelluccio, Stéphane. *Le Garde-Meuble de la Couronne et ses intendants du XVI⁰ au XVIII⁰ siècle*. Paris, 2004.

Castelluccio 2013 Castelluccio, Stéphane. *Le Goût pour les porcelaines de Chine et du Japon à Paris aux XVII⁰ et XVIII⁰ siècles*. Saint-Rémy-en-l'Eau, 2013.

Castelluccio 2014 Castelluccio, Stéphane. *Le Prince et le marchand: Le commerce de luxe chez les marchands merciers parisiens pendant le règne de Louis XIV*. Paris, 2014.

Castelluccio 2019a Castelluccio, Stéphane. *Le Goût pour les laques d'Orient en France aux XVII⁰ et XVIII⁰ siècles*. Saint-Rémy-en-l'Eau, 2019.

Castelluccio 2019b Castelluccio, Stéphane. "Louis XIV, le Siam et la Chine: séduire et être séduit." *Extrême-Orient Extrême-Occident*, no. 43 (2019): 25–44.

Castelluccio 2022 Castelluccio, Stéphane. *Le Garde-Meuble de la Couronne et ses intendants du XVI⁰ au XVIII⁰ siècle*. 2nd ed. Paris, 2022.

***Catalogue de tableaux* 1803** *Catalogue de tableaux . . . par les plus grands maîtres des écoles d'Italie, de France, de Flandre et de Hollande . . . porcelaines du Japon, de la Chine, de Saxe et de Sèvres; riches meubles de Boulle, etc.* Sale cat. A. Paillet et H. Delaroche, Paris, April 18, 1803.

Chuang 2020 Chuang, Grace. "Bernard (II) Vanrisamburgh, Master Cabinetmaker in Eighteenth-Century Paris." PhD diss., Institute of Fine Arts, New York, 2020.

Coquery 2004 Coquery, Natacha. "The Language of Success: Marketing and Distributing Semi-Luxury Goods in Eighteenth-Century Paris." *Journal of Design History* 17, no. 1 (2004): 71–89.

Coquery 2006 Coquery, Natacha. *Tenir boutique à Paris au XVIII⁰ siècle: Luxe et demi-luxe*. Paris, 2006.

Courajod 1873 Courajod, Louis, ed. *Livre journal de Lazare Duvaux, marchand-bijoutier ordinaire du roy, 1748–1758*. 2 vols. Paris, 1873.

Dell 1992 Dell, Theodore, ed. *Furniture in The Frick Collection: Italian and French Renaissance, French 18th and 19th Centuries*. Pt. 1. Vol. 5. New York, 1992.

Dessert 1984 Dessert, Daniel. *Argent, pouvoir et société au Grand Siècle*. Paris, 1984.

Dessert 2012 Dessert, Daniel. *L'Argent du sel, le sel de l'argent*. Paris, 2012.

Durand 1971 Durand, Yves. *Les Fermiers généraux au XVIIIᵉ siècle*. Paris, 1971.

Eriksen 1962 Eriksen, Svend. "Marigny and Le Goût Grec." *Burlington Magazine*, no. 104 (March 1962): 96–101.

Finlay 2019 Finlay, John. "Henri Bertin and Louis XV's Gifts to the Qianlong Emperor." *Extrême-Orient Extrême-Occident*, no. 43 (2019): 93–112.

Fuhring 1999 Fuhring, Peter. *Juste-Aurèle Meissonnier: Un génie du rococo*. Turin and London, 1999.

Fuzelier 1735 Fuzelier, Louis. *Les Indes galantes, ballet heroique représenté par l'Academie royale de Musique pour la premiere fois le mardy 23. août 1735*. Paris, 1735.

Giraud 2022 Giraud, Paul. "Pierre Macret (1723–1806): Marchand mercier et ébéniste privilégié du roi suivant la Cour." Thesis, École du Louvre, 2022.

Glorieux 2002 Glorieux, Guillaume. *À l'enseigne de Gersaint: Edme-François Gersaint, marchand d'art sur le pont Notre-Dame (1694–1750)*. Seyssel, 2002.

Le Rond d'Alembert and Diderot 1765 Le Rond d'Alembert, Jean, and Denis Diderot, eds. *Encyclopédie, ou Dictionnaire raisonné des arts et des métiers par une société de gens de lettres*. Vol. 10. Paris, 1765.

Mercure de France **1724** *Mercure de France dédié au Roy*, July 1724.

Mercure de France **1742** *Mercure de France, dédié au Roy*, vol. 2 (June 1742).

Mercure de France **1765** *Mercure de France, dédié au Roi*, March 1765.

Paris 2014 Anne Foray-Carlier and Monika Kopplin, eds. *Les Secrets de la laque française: Le vernis Martin*. Exh. cat. Paris (Musée des Arts Décoratifs), 2014.

Paris 2018 Rose-Marie Herda-Mousseaux, ed. *La Fabrique du luxe: Les marchands merciers parisiens au XVIIIᵉ siècle*. Exh. cat. Paris (Musée Cognacq-Jay), 2018.

Perrin 1993 Perrin, Christiane. *François-Thomas Germain: Orfèvre des rois*. Saint-Rémy-en-l'Eau, 1993.

Poumarède 2009 Poumarède, Géraud. "Les envoyés ottomans à la cour de France: d'une représentation controversée à l'exaltation d'une alliance." In *Turcs et turqueries (XVIᵉ–XVIIIᵉ siècles)*, edited by Lucien Bély, 63–95. Paris, 2009.

Poumarède 2020 Poumarède, Géraud. *L'Empire de Venise et les Turcs, XVIᵉ–XVIIᵉ siècle*. Paris, 2020.

Pradère 1989a Pradère, Alexandre. *Les Ébénistes français de Louis XIV à la Révolution*. Paris, 1989.

Pradère 1989b Pradère, Alexandre. "Madame de Pompadour et le goût grec." *Connaissance des Arts*, no. 454 (December 1989): 106–9.

Pradère 2003 Pradère, Alexandre. *Charles Cressent: Sculpteur, ébéniste du Régent*. Paris, 2003.

Pruchnicki 2013 Pruchnicki, Vincent. *Arnouville: Le château des Machault au XVIIIᵉ siècle*. Paris, 2013.

"Relation" 1725 "Relation de l'arrivée en France de quatre Sauvages de Missicipi . . ." *Mercure de France dédié au Roi*, vol. 1 (December 1725): 2827–59.

Roche 1989 Roche, Daniel. *La Culture des apparences: Une histoire du vêtement (XVIIᵉ–XVIIIᵉ siècle)*. Paris, 1989.

Roche 1997 Roche, Daniel. *Histoire des choses banales: Naissance de la société de consommation dans les sociétés traditionnelles, XVIIIᵉ–XIXᵉ siècle*. Paris, 1997.

Rochebrune 2019 Rochebrune, Marie-Laure de. "Les porcelaines de Sèvres envoyées en guise de cadeaux diplomatiques à l'empereur de Chine par les souverains français dans la seconde moitié du XVIIIe siècle." *Extrême-Orient Extrême-Occident*, no. 43 (2019): 81–92.

Roubo 1774 Roubo, André Jacob. *L'Art du menuisier ébéniste*. Paris, 1774.

Sanson 2016 Sanson, Aurélie. "Les figures de l'étranger dans les *Mémoires* de Saint-Simon: comment peut-on être étranger à ma cour?" *Bulletin du Centre de recherche du château de Versailles*, no. 11 (2016), https://journals.openedition.org/crcv/17749

Sargentson 1996 Sargentson, Carolyn. *Merchants and Luxury Markets: The Marchands Merciers of Eighteenth-Century Paris*. London, 1996.

Smentek 2019 Smentek, Kristel. "Chinoiseries for the Qing: A French Gift of Tapestries to the Qianlong Emperor." *Journal of Early Modern History*, no. 20 (2019): 93–112.

"Spectacles" 1725 "Spectacles." *Mercure de France, dédié au Roy*, vol. 2 (September 1725): 2274–76.

"Spectacles" 1735a "Spectacles." *Mercure de France, dédié au Roy*, August 1735, 1825–52.

"Spectacles" 1735b "Spectacles." *Mercure de France, dédié au Roy*, September 1735, 2035–61.

"Spectacles" 1736a "Spectacles." *Mercure de France, dédié au Roy*, February 1736, 328–58.

"Spectacles" 1736b "Spectacles." *Mercure de France, dédié au Roy*, March 1736, 534–50.

"Suite de l'Ambassade" 1743 "Suite de l'Ambassade solemnelle de la Porte Ottomane à la Cour de France, 1743." *Mercure de France, dédié au Roi*, vol. 2 (December 1743): 2763–94.

"Supplication" 1754 [Charles-Nicolas Cochin] "Supplication aux Orfèvres, Ciseleurs, Sculpteurs en bois pour les appartemens & autres, par une société d'Artistes." *Mercure de France, dédié au Roi*, vol. 2 (December 1754): 178–87.

Veinstein 2014 Veinstein, Gilles, ed. *Mehmed Effendi. Le Paradis des infidèles: Un ambassadeur ottoman en France sous la Régence*. Paris, 2014.

Vente de fond 1764
"Vente de fond de boutique en sousbail Bernard Vanrisamburg . . . a leur fils." Sale, Paris, October 18, 1764. Archives Nationales de France, Minutier Central, XXVIII, 389.

Verlet 1958 Verlet, Pierre. "Le commerce des objets d'art et les marchands merciers à Paris au XVIIIe siècle." *Annales Économies, sociétés, civilisations* 13, no. 1 (1958): 10–29.

Versailles 2014a Daniel Alcouffe et al., eds. *18e aux sources du design: Chefs d'œuvre du mobilier, 1650 à 1790*. Exh. cat. Versailles (Château de Versailles), 2014.

Versailles 2014b Marie-Laure de Rochebrune, ed. *La Chine à Versailles: Art et diplomatie au XVIIIe siècle*. Exh. cat. Versailles (Château de Versailles), 2014.

Versailles 2017 Danièlle Kisluk-Grosheide and Bertrand Rondot, eds. *Visiteurs de Versailles. Voyageurs, princes, ambassadeurs, 1682–1789*. Exh. cat. Versailles (Château de Versailles), 2017.

Vignon 2015 Vignon, Charlotte. *The Frick Collection Decorative Arts Handbook*. New York, 2015.

Vittet 2009 Vittet, Jean. "Le marchand Thomas-Joachim Hébert (1687–1773) et l'ébénisterie de son temps." In *Le commerce du luxe à Paris aux XVIIe et XVIIIe siècles*, edited by Stéphane Castelluccio, 177–97. Bern, 2009.

Williams 2014 Williams, Haydn, ed. *Turquerie: An Eighteenth-Century European Fantasy*. London, 2014.

Wolvesperges 2000 Wolvesperges, Thibaut. *Le Meuble français en laque au XVIIIe siècle*. Brussels, 2000.

Zhao and Simon 2019 Zhao, Bing, and Fabien Simon. "Les cadeaux diplomatiques entre la Chine et l'Europe aux XVIIe–XVIIIe siècles. Pratiques et enjeux." *Extrême-Orient Extrême-Occident*, no. 43 (2019): 5–24.